CAMBRIDGE LIBRARY COLLECTION

Books of enduring scholarly value

East and South-East Asian History

This series focuses on East and South-East Asia from the early modern period to the end of the Victorian era. It includes contemporary accounts of European encounters with the civilisations of China, Japan and South-East Asia from the time of the Jesuit missions and the East India companies to the Chinese revolution of 1911.

The Past and Future of British Relations in China

In 1860, naval officer Sherard Osborn (1822–75), a veteran of both Opium Wars, published this collection of remarks and predictions on Chinese affairs in relation to British imperial interests. Osborn writes in forthright style of his time in the East and his negative experiences of Chinese diplomacy to support his view that 'the European has ever to use force rather than argument to obtain his ends in China, be they however moderate, however just'. He also sets out some advice on how to prevent British smugglers from taking advantage of the Chinese. A number of Osborn's other publications are also reissued in the Cambridge Library Collection, including *Stray Leaves from an Arctic Journal* (1852), *The Discovery of the North-West Passage by H.M.S. Investigator* (1856), and *The Career, Last Voyage, and Fate of Captain Sir John Franklin* (1860).

T0382120

Cambridge University Press has long been a pioneer in the reissuing of out-of-print titles from its own backlist, producing digital reprints of books that are still sought after by scholars and students but could not be reprinted economically using traditional technology. The Cambridge Library Collection extends this activity to a wider range of books which are still of importance to researchers and professionals, either for the source material they contain, or as landmarks in the history of their academic discipline.

Drawing from the world-renowned collections in the Cambridge University Library and other partner libraries, and guided by the advice of experts in each subject area, Cambridge University Press is using state-of-the-art scanning machines in its own Printing House to capture the content of each book selected for inclusion. The files are processed to give a consistently clear, crisp image, and the books finished to the high quality standard for which the Press is recognised around the world. The latest print-on-demand technology ensures that the books will remain available indefinitely, and that orders for single or multiple copies can quickly be supplied.

The Cambridge Library Collection brings back to life books of enduring scholarly value (including out-of-copyright works originally issued by other publishers) across a wide range of disciplines in the humanities and social sciences and in science and technology.

The Past and Future
of British Relations
in China

SHERARD OSBORN

CAMBRIDGE
UNIVERSITY PRESS

University Printing House, Cambridge, CB2 8BS, United Kingdom

Cambridge University Press is part of the University of Cambridge.
It furthers the University's mission by disseminating knowledge in the pursuit of
education, learning and research at the highest international levels of excellence.

www.cambridge.org
Information on this title: www.cambridge.org/9781108071734

© in this compilation Cambridge University Press 2014

This edition first published 1860
This digitally printed version 2014

ISBN 978-1-108-07173-4 Paperback

This book reproduces the text of the original edition. The content and language reflect
the beliefs, practices and terminology of their time, and have not been updated.

Cambridge University Press wishes to make clear that the book, unless originally published
by Cambridge, is not being republished by, in association or collaboration with,
or with the endorsement or approval of, the original publisher or its successors in title.

The original edition of this book contains a number of colour plates,
which have been reproduced in black and white. Colour versions of these
images can be found online at www.cambridge.org/9781108071734

THE

PAST AND FUTURE

OF

BRITISH RELATIONS IN CHINA

THE

PAST AND FUTURE

OF

BRITISH RELATIONS IN CHINA

BY

CAPTAIN SHERARD OSBORN, C.B.

ROYAL NAVY

AUTHOR OF "A CRUISE IN JAPANESE WATERS,"
ETC.

WILLIAM BLACKWOOD AND SONS
EDINBURGH AND LONDON
MDCCCLX

PREFACE.

A PREFACE is seldom read : mine shall be a brief one. The sad lack of sound information evinced in the late debates upon China, and the incontestable fact that the opinions of the majority were based not upon historical and commercial data, but simply upon the statements of certain special interests, or factions, convinced me that it was high time that he who had any information to give upon the past or future of China, should now speak, or henceforth be silent.

A portion of the following pages appeared as articles in *Blackwood*, and some of the information was laid before my colleagues of the Royal Geographical Society. I have, however, added largely to both, and brought the facts up to the latest dates, erasing all strictures which, written on the spur of the moment, might have been objectionable in a reprint, or would have appeared to be malicious.

In giving the public the fruits of my experience and observation gleaned during two wars in China, I have pandered to neither clique, office, nor cloth, and striven to think and write as one who consulted alone the glory and interests of his Queen and Country.

SHERARD OSBORN,
Captain.

London, *August* 1860.

CONTENTS.

CHAPTER I.

REMARKS ON CHINESE REASONING — H. M. S. FURIOUS AT
SHANGHAI—PROCEED TO THE GULF OF PECHELI—THE
PEIHO RIVER, ,.. 1-70

CHAPTER II.

OUR FUTURE RELATIONS WITH CHINA, ... 71-113

CHAPTER III.

WAR AND PROGRESS IN CHINA, ...114-179

APPENDIX.

MEMORANDA EXTRACTED FROM "TRAVELS IN CHINA" (BY SIR
JOHN BARROW, BART.), RELATIVE TO THE PEIHO RIVER
AND THE PROVINCE OF PECHELI, BETWEEN TAKU AND
PEKIN, ...180 184

ILLUSTRATIONS.

MAP OF CHINA.
THE RIVER PEIHO, OR TIENTSIN-HOA, FROM THE ENTRANCE
TO TIENTSIN.
THE SAME, FROM TIENTSIN TO PEKIN.

THE PAST AND FUTURE

OF

BRITISH RELATIONS IN CHINA.

———◆———

CHAPTER I.

REMARKS ON CHINESE REASONING — H.M.S. FURIOUS AT
SHANGHAI — PROCEED TO THE GULF OF PECHELI — THE
PEIHO RIVER.

WHEN an Englishman has reasoned upon any Chinese
question, the best thing for him to do, having arrived
at his conclusion, is to say, " But the Emperor, mandarins, and Chinamen, will come to exactly an opposite decision, and act accordingly." My experience
of China, extending through two wars, as they have
been called, amounts to the above statement. I never
remember any European who took an European, and,
I grant, rational view of China, who was in the end
right. I might quote blue-books and works without
number to prove my assertion ; and go back as far

A

as the year 1839, to show how everybody guessed wrong, simply through their not being able to think as a Chinaman thinks. But such a host of proof exists within the last few months of this melancholy fact, that a mere summary of them will suffice to show the grounds upon which I rest so broad an assertion.

In 1856, Hong-Kong thought one thing, Canton did exactly contrary; Sir John Bowring came to one conclusion, Governor-General Yeh to the opposite. The allied diplomatists, generals, admirals, and staffs, have thought certain measures would bring about certain concessions, but up to this day, the spring of 1858, all have been utterly mistaken ; and yet they would all, these Europeans, be wise men in any other country except China.

We Europeans saw Governor-General Yeh and his fellow-imperialists beset with difficulties from rebellion in 1856 ; we fancied their arrogance must have abated under such circumstances, and that the Chinese authorities would wink at the fraud under which native vessels were availing themselves of the British flag—a mere screen for piracy and smuggling. The Chinese authorities seized a vessel and insulted the flag.

We Europeans thought the insult to the flag a good opportunity for humbling Governor-General Yeh, by trying to induce him to receive British civil authorities in a personal interview, and in demanding redress for the insult, we coupled reparation with an old treaty-right of entering the city of Canton.

Governor-General Yeh saw at once through our motives, and, cleverly separating the two questions, he offered reparation for the one error, but clearly showed that because he had inadvertently insulted our flag when it was illegally flown, that was no reason why he should allow us to perpetrate an act which, in every Chinaman's eyes, was an insult to his sovereign and country.

We Europeans fancied that if the prestige of Canton never having been entered by a foreigner was broken through, the whole prejudice would fall to the ground. We had seen that city lately subjected to a siege by the Taeping forces, and rebellion rife in the surrounding country. We reasoned that Governor-General Yeh must be in the minority, his power very diminished, and that before the imperial authority was again fully re-established, we could carry our point by entering the city of Canton as victors. Hostilities commenced, and Governor-General Yeh suffered one defeat; a small body of English sailors and soldiers did march through a breach into the city, and eventually marched back again. Every Chinaman of Canton, contrary to our expectation, rushed to the support of Governor-General Yeh. He turned the tables upon us. We had again come to wrong conclusions. He actually burnt down the British factories whilst our forces were in and around them; and instead of our succeeding in making him receive our representative at Hong-Kong, much less the consuls or vice-consuls of Canton—instead of our establishing a precedent for right of entry into Canton—and instead of our finding Governor-General Yeh so weak and humbled that he was ready to do all we wished, or yield to our threats — we found him a most rampant, intractable wearer of coral buttons and peacock's feathers, and, in Eastern parlance, we Britons ate more dirt during twelve months than it would be pleasant or profitable to dwell upon.

Well, the mistakes of Hong-Kong led our Government at home into the mess. Of course we were not going to stand a thrashing from Governor-General Yeh, or going to allow him to correct the mental hallucinations of our Hong-Kong compatriots, by a free administration of arsenical paste in their morning rolls; and the erection of triumphal arches recording the retreat of the British forces, the failure of our attempts to coerce Yeh, and enter that odoriferous City of Rams, was not to be tolerated. Great Britain had to interfere, not only to retrieve her damaged prestige—a damage simply arising from our reasoning having led us to wrong conclusions as to what Yeh and his supporters would do under certain circumstances—but physical force had to be applied *to compel the Chinaman to do what we thought right!*

We set about it in a strange manner, I acknowledge. However, let us suppose that the burnings of British factories, insults to British flags, imprisonments of British subjects, poisonings of Hong-Kong residents, had anything to do with Louis Napoleon, or the propagation of the faith of the Scarlet Lady—and that John Bull could no longer punish the Emperor of China without the aid and counsel of his friend across the water in peg-top trousers—let us suppose all this, and, by some additional stretch of the imagination, fancy that British commerce, Popery, and Napoleon III. had common ends in view. Such being the case, our ministers at home, and representatives about to proceed to the East, naturally sat in council, and framed instructions for a plan of operations based upon what they thought would bring the Chinese to their senses. Then read those instructions (see *Blue-Book* of Lord Elgin's Embassy) ; note how they had entirely to be set aside ; note how our ambassadors had constantly to change their policy from one of thought and diplomacy or reason to action and application of brute-force; note how when force was not immediately applied, it had always to be threatened ; and I cannot help thinking it will be allowed that force rather than argument, necessity rather than conviction, is the only rule by which a Chinaman can be made to agree with a European.

The spring of 1858, a year after our Government took the affair in hand, still found us realising that fact. Throughout the previous autumn and winter we were constantly expecting exactly the opposite results from the action of the allied forces to those which actually accrued.

When the force first arrived at Hong-Kong, all those who had hitherto been constantly wrong in their opinions, persisted that the affair could be arranged on the spot; that through Canton, Pekin was to be acted upon; that directly Yeh saw we were in earnest he would yield—that the Emperor would be rid of an official who brought European armies upon him in addition to the vast hordes of rebels then traversing the country; that it was a local question, not an imperial one : and, strange to relate, in spite of the experience of 1856, Hong-Kong had its way, and by the month of December a huge allied force was assembled in the waters of the Pearl River to fight out the question by a simple entry into the city of Canton. Lord Elgin and Baron Gros now commenced to think to reason, and, in short, to treat a Chinaman as if he was a European. They wrote to Yeh, and so did Mr Reid the American minister, who was a neutral. Belligerents or neutrals, it was immaterial; Yeh, the personification of the Chinese intellect, differed with them all—negotiations failed, ultimatums failed, and then we acted. We captured Can-

ton—a childish feat of arms, pleasantly recorded in that
very pleasant book about China, written by my friend
George Wingrove Cooke. We took three parts of
the circumference of the walls, and waited some
days, thinking Yeh would make a sign of surrender.
No, he sat in his yamun; if you wanted him, you
must fetch him. It was said he would commit sui-
cide, that a Chinaman could not outlive dishonour.
Again wrong. He was captured; he did not swallow
poison. We garrisoned Canton; wise men said it
would convince every Chinaman of our prowess. No
such thing. It was all "one twice-eye pigeon," a
trick: we had not dared to attack Yeh and his braves
in the front; and we climbed up on the east when he
expected us on the west! Even the Chinamen in our
colonies, who ought to have better appreciated our
power, seemed to think that the best proof of our
being unable to take any more of their cities, was that
we *only* captured Canton with such a force, and after
so much noise, fuss, and preparation! Forbearance!
you said. He never heard of the word in trade or
business; it never was known to an Asiatic; he
understood it not, except in this way: if a strong man
with a stick met a weak one ladened with silver, the
strong man would strike the other, take away all he
had, but not kill him outright, policy rendered it ad-
visable not to be a murderer as well as a robber; that

was all the forbearance of which a Chinaman had ever heard or known.

However, Canton was ours, so far as its walls and silent streets went; and Yeh was ours, so far as he went. We enjoyed our New-Year's revels, and thought of the confusion and humiliation of Emperor and Court. Yeh was to be repudiated; our treaty-right to enter Canton recognised; commissioners would hasten down to try and conciliate us on the spot; and a new tariff, or new treaty, would follow.

January, February, and March nigh passed, not the slightest notice was taken of the Allies, Canton, or poor Yeh! It was very evident that north we must go; so a threat was sent off to Pekin, with a suggestion that our visit there might be warded off by commissioners being sent to Shanghai. Yeh, the redoubtable, was offered up, a stout victim to the difference of opinion between Hong-Kong and Canton. A summer cruise in a cabin of a steam-sloop to that salubrious spot, Calcutta, must have prepared him for the Buddhist purgatory of his faith. And, twelve months after leaving England, Lord Elgin was carried in my frigate into Shanghai, to find another supposition as to what Emperor or Court would do—a simple mistake. There were no commissioners there, and there would be none sent—until Emperor and Court were beaten into doing as he desired.

Now, it is not only in diplomacy, foreign policy, and

public points that we thus ever are at variance with
Chinamen, but I firmly believe that, in all matters,
however trivial, we and these people ever differ. I
can hardly remember an instance of my going to a
Chinaman, and expressing an opinion, that his reply
did not commence with the words, "My no thinkee
so!" and then, in his way, he generally told you that
exactly the contrary would be the case. If the question
was a Chinese one, he was generally right, unless we
used force, and made things come round to our view of
the case. In short, the European in China appears to
me to be ever singing a song about the Flowery Land
and its people, to which the native, standing by, strikes
in with a chorus of "My no thinkee so!"

Here, in March 1858, was another instance of the
same thing. Diplomatists, generals, and admirals had
just sung their song of triumph over Canton. We
were to have all we wanted; we became humane; and,
as is usual after perpetrating all sorts of violence, very
conscientious. Poor dear Chinaman! no more blood-
shed—no more robbery—no more frauds upon your
revenue. You shall be humble, we will be generous—
but, botheration! here had this pig-headed Hienfung
the First again proclaimed, "My no thinkee so!"
He would have none of us, our treaties, or representa-
tions. What! because we had surreptitiously entered
Canton, and his officers, knowing that two men could

not be in one place at the same time, had wisely
vacated it—was that a reason why he should depart
from a policy anterior to the flood? Because we had
Canton, was that a reason why he should run away
from Pekin? Was not his land swarming with rebels?
—his coast with pirates?—and yet his authority un-
shaken? Because two buccaneers more, named Elee-
Kee and Tolo (Elgin and Gros), seized a fusty city
called Canton, and carried off a red-buttoned mandarin,
was that going to frighten Emperor and Councillors?
Let such children go and fire rockets at the moon!
"You no can go that Pekin side!" chuckled your
Chinese acquaintance in Shanghai or Hong-Kong.
What he said, though totally contrary to all our ideas
of sense and reason, was exactly what Emperor, Court,
and the people believed.

What can you do with such a people? Either one of
two things: Leave them alone to exult in their obstinate
ignorance, or make them by force yield to your view
of the case. Necessity compels us to adopt the latter
course. We cannot exist without tea and silk; we want
that huge market of four hundred millions for our
manufactures; the exchequers of Britain and India
need the revenue already derived from the trade between us. But, instead of taking one or other of these
two courses, we try to combine them. We want the
Chinaman to act as we think best, without using

force, or without apparently consulting our own interests. The result is constant bickerings, and ultimate use of large force; whereas, if you simply started upon the ground of, You must do so and so, the Chinese intellect would appreciate the consequences, and yield. *We* are barbarians, and unreasonable under all circumstances; nothing we can say or do will alter that opinion of us; do, therefore, what is right, and merely consult our own consciences and the interests of our country.

We always come to this in the long-run in China— the sword, or a threat of the sword, has invariably decided every dispute, however trivial, with these people. Turn to the consular records at the five ports: they are civil establishments, but when did they succeed in carrying a point without threatening force? Think how many times the Bocca Tigris has been stormed, how many times Canton has been attacked by us, and how often the threat of stopping the imperial grain fleet has been used, and it will, I think, be generally acknowledged, that in the end we have had to say to John Chinaman, "You must do so and so," instead of hoping and begging he would act as we thought right. European diplomacy in China amounts to a just appreciation of what is right, what is to the interest of European civilisation, and then a skilful application of force, not reason.

The spring of 1858 saw a fresh exemplification of this

law : we were obliged to make Emperor and mandarin do what we thought right, by the employment of force. An unsatisfactory reply from Pekin made the ambassador sigh for the persuasive powers of a flotilla of gunboats which the ministry at home had wisely given him to enforce his arguments; and sword, not pen, was again the means by which Lord Elgin found himself compelled to carry conviction to the reason of a Chinaman.

The Furious had already had for some months the honour of carrying about the British ambassador and suite in Chinese waters; and replete with interest as had already been our cruise in the gallant frigate, the new ground upon which we were shortly to enter rendered the proposed voyage very exciting, and all our preparations for a prolonged stay in the Gulf of Pecheli were expeditiously and zealously completed. Apart from mere curiosity, the importance of reaching the near vicinity of the Chinese capital, and of placing the ambassador in a position to dictate his own terms, was evident; and none but those grown blind by gazing at Canton could help seeing that it was unworthy of Great Britain to be merely squabbling with the militia of a wretched Chinese city, two thousand miles distant from the centre of government.

We had taken care to start from Hong-Kong at such a time as to give the Furious the best chance of escaping the bad weather likely to occur about the vernal

equinox, and were enabled to visit Swatow, Amoy, Fu-
chow-fu, Ningpo, Shapu, and the whole Chusan Archipelago, without encountering a single double-reef topsail breeze to mar the interest of the cruise, or to prevent us acquiring that *local information from personal
observation* of the resources and capabilities of the many
places visited, which, after all, is worth far more than
reading whole libraries of travel or history.

Of the queen of Central China, the good city of
Shanghai, I need not say more, while so much has
been written and is being written of it, than that sixteen years ago (in 1842), I was one of some half-dozen
English boats' crews, under the Commodore, R. B.
Watson, C.B., and part of the fleet of Admiral Sir W.
Parker, G.C.B., who first burst upon the Chinese quietude of its existence as the pioneers of a new order of
things; and I am sure not the most sanguine among us
could have anticipated that such a magnificent European colony would have been created in so short a space
of time. Who could have foretold that where no foreign
keel had ever before floated, an import and export
trade in European bottoms, amounting to the value of
(£26,774,018) twenty-six millions seven hundred and
seventy-four thousand odd pounds ! would *now* exist,*

* The Custom-House returns for 1857, published at Shanghai by the
head of the Anglo-Chinese Customs, Mr H. N. Lay, show for 1857,
£16,239,696, general trade; opium, £5,243,288; treasure, £4,846,260;
copper coin, £444,774. Total, £26,774,018.

and that at the same time the native trade and native craft would show no apparent diminution. Yet it is so. Where a low, unhealthy marsh, dotted with squalid Chinese abodes, only then met the eye, such a quay or bund is now seen as would put those who live on the banks of Father Thames to the blush!—handsome houses, gardens, yachts, mail-steamers and steam-tugs —a thousand indications, in short, of the wealth and prosperity of a great commercial community.

The naval officer, contemplating such a scene of prosperity and wealth, replete with high promise to all the world, suddenly created on the footprints left by his profession, may, at any rate, without egotism, say that its labours have not been in vain; and as I turned my back upon Shanghai towards the fresh unbroken ground north of the Yang-tze, the hope naturally arose that our coming labours might be equally prolific in benefits to Great Britain and China.

The weather, whilst we had been in Shanghai, was beautiful; the north-east monsoon had lost its keen edge, while the sun was not yet too hot to wear blue clothing, or forbid brisk exercise. Spurts of wind from south and south-east had occurred for the last month, and, taking advantage of it, two divisions of the Chinese grain junks had already started for Pekin: the first division, with some eight thousand tons of rice, had arrived, we were told, at the capital; the

second division started about the time we arrived in the
river ; and when the Chinese officials at Shanghai
learned the possibility of hostilities, the greatest anxiety
was expressed lest we should occasion a famine in the
North and in Pekin by intercepting these supplies.
The rebellion in the valley of the Yang-tze-kiang, the
occupation of Ching-kiang-fu on the Great Canal, and
the unruly Hoang-ho, or Yellow River, having left its
bed and taken some other course, had all combined to
force the old canal traffic between Northern and Southern China into a coasting trade ; and it said a good deal
for the energy and nautical enterprise of the Chinese
that they had thus quickly adapted themselves to circumstances, and undertaken to convey not only luxuries, but actually food, to the northern provinces, in the
same description of vessels with which I perfectly remember seeing them navigate the smooth waters of the
Yang-tze-kiang in former days.   With such a people I
maintain it is folly to say that they will " break before
they will bend."   They are only Asiatics ; *make them
do a thing*—compel them to advance—and they will do
it as well as any of us ; but consult their prejudices, or
their ease, and good-bye to any change or advancement.
Bear that in mind—treat them as children ; make
them do what we know is for their benefit, as well as
our own, and all difficulties with China are at an end.

After waiting at Shanghai from March 25th to April

8th for the gunboats to arrive, Lord Elgin induced the Captain of the Pique to proceed northwards at once, and a few days afterwards, April 10, 1858, the Furious took the Slaney gunboat in tow, and weighed from Shanghai to proceed down the Yang-tze-kiang River for the same destination.

Between the Amherst Rocks, at the northern entrance of the Yang-tze and Shantung Point, we were, generally speaking, in smooth water, although sharp breezes of short duration sprang up alternately from north-north-east and south ; the latter bringing with it a low white mist, through which the quaint hulls and quainter cut sails of many Chinese junks were constantly seen. The majority of these vessels were recognised by their peculiar form to be from Shanghai or the Yang-tze-kiang, whilst here and there those of Fu-chow-fu, Amoy, and Canton, were distinguished by certain forms of hull, cut of sail, or eccentricity in their paint ; for it is as easy to recognise the junks belonging to the different provinces of the seaboard of China—indeed, to distinguish the fishing-boats of one portion of the coast from those of another—as it is when running up the English Channel to know a Cawsand Bay smack from an Isle of Wight wherry, or Brighton cobble. Be it remembered, however, that it is only in the external form and paint of his junk, or cut of his sails, that the Chinaman of the South differs from him of the

North. In all the internal fittings and nautical gear there is not the slightest difference. In all sea-going junks the rudder lifts or lowers at pleasure, the tiller is equally long, the sails are always lug-sails, whether the craft be of one or one hundred tons, and the wooden anchor and coir-cable work upon immutable principles, which would delight those ancient mariners of Europe who weep over the departed days of hemp cables and shingle ballast. The unconservative departure from certain laws which the Chinaman allows himself in junk-building, is, however, of this much use to the European, that in thick weather our opium-clippers and packets, running up and down the coast, often know they are off a certain port or district by the appearance of the fishing-junks working about in the offing.

The uniformity of the soundings, as well as nature of the bottom, the Furious sailed over in the 360 miles of sea intervening between the mouths of the Yang-tze River and Shantung Point, proved we were merely travelling over a submarine region, formed by the alluvial deposits of those twin giants—the Hoang-ho and Yang-tze-kiang. It was deeply interesting to think that at some future day the plain beneath our keel would, by accumulated deposits, rise to low-water mark, and then, like much of the adjacent coast of China, be immediately seized upon by swarming Chinese, be diked, cultivated, populated, and added to

B

that already wonderful region known as the Great
Plain of China—an event which, judging by the rapid
formation of Tsung-ming, Bush Island, and other spots
in this neighbourhood, is not so far distant as many
might suppose.   After a run of nearly 400 miles on a
north course, we reached the Shantung promontory,
and entered what has been called the Yellow Sea,
though I know not with what justice, for its waters
struck me to be of a purer pale sea-green than those of
the region we had left behind us, or those of the Gulf
of Pecheli, which we afterwards entered.   There was
now a decided decrease in the temperature of the air,
and at nights it was even in our cabins as low as 58°
Fahr.   Daylight of April 13th found us off Alceste
Island, and as we steered to the westward for the Straits
of Mia-tao, a cold south-east breeze from the high lands
of Shantung rolled back the night mists from hill and
valley, displaying under a rising sun a glorious and
striking panorama, which, though perhaps not so rich
as that valley of the Yang-tze in which we had been
so long to the southward, was far more preferable to
the eye.   Leu-cung Island, and Wei-hai-wei harbour,
were soon passed ; and it took us all the forenoon to
cross the broad unsheltered bay, at the eastern horn of
which stands the now important city of Che-chow-fu.
Great numbers of junks were working close along shore:
most of them, possibly from fear of us, passed inside

the numerous islets forming the Che-fu harbour of our charts.

This anchorage, of which we have a survey by Lieutenant D. Ross of the Bombay marine, made in the year 1816, only affords partial shelter from north-east and east gales, which are, I should think, those most to be avoided in this sea. A French frigate subsequently anchored in the bay, and in a north-east breeze pitched bows under in a tremendous sea, with 180 fathoms of cable on a single anchor. Outside, and bearing about north-east by east three-quarters of a mile distant from the outer island, called North Island, we observed breakers which are not marked in the charts, showing that although the survey is generally correct, so far as cross-bearings and transits of the points would allow us to form an idea, it must have been hastily done. From Che-fu Point to Teng-chow-fu, a large city thirty miles W.N.W. of the former, the land was very picturesque, the coast slightly indented, but with no appearance of secure harbours. The scenery of Shantung, the peculiar form of the hills, and the natural or artificial tumuli which appeared to crown their summits, or rise from the level plateaus, recalled strongly to my mind the peninsulas of Taman and Kertch, on the shores of the Black Sea. The resemblance led to speculation in my mind as to the connection between two points so far apart upon the globe's surface. Both were in

Asia; both spots were on the southern edge of the
great Tartarian region, and in about the same degree
of north latitude; over both, at no very remote period,
nomadic tribes of the same great family had wandered
as conquerors or fugitives, and erected those silent yet
expressive tumuli, either as tokens of their sovereignty,
or in barbaric honour of departed warrior chiefs. Those
in the far West were now in the hands of the warlike
Russian, to be hollowed out into Mamelons and Mala-
koffs for the good of the orthodox faith; these before
us in the East had been seized upon by the Chinese, a
far more practical race, who, alas for the poetry of the
act! turned these chambers, fashioned for the post-
mortem revels of the mounted Viking of Tartary, into
lime and brick-kilns! if not yet viler purposes.

Ugly shoals and broken water showed on either side
of the city of Teng-chow-fu,* and as the Furious rattled
along under steam and sail, the extensive battlements
of the city struck even those who were fresh from the
great Chinese towns of Canton and Shanghai, as enclosing an area larger than any before seen. Teng-
chow-fu stands upon a level plateau which rises somewhat abruptly from the sea to a height of a hundred

---

* It is hopeless to profess to be correct about the pronunciation or
orthography of names of places in China, so long as those learned in
such matters differ in opinion. The Admiralty Chart calls it "Teng-
chu-fu;" Lord Macartney writes it "Ten-choo-foo;" Mr Williams, the
American, in his map spells it "Tang-chau-fu;" and so on.

feet or so. Within its walls, and at the north-west angle, is a conical hill, crowned with a temple—an admirable position for a citadel. Not far in the rear the lofty hills of Shangking are seen, and the ground rises on the eastern and western sides of the city; indeed, in a military point of view, the walls are dominated by a ridge of hills running out to the east, and from the extreme point of which the Gulf of Pecheli may be said to commence.

The best information we possess of Teng-chow-fu, and that meagre enough, is to be found in the voluminous narrative of Lord Macartney's embassy to China in 1793. It will be one of the new ports open for European commerce, and likely to play an important part as the emporium of Northern China; I shall therefore take the liberty of briefly transcribing the remarks contained in that work.

After mentioning that the walls of Teng-chow-fu enclosed more ground than was occupied by houses—a remark, by the by, applicable to all Chinese cities—the writer proceeds to say—

" The bay, or rather road, of Teng-chow-fu, not only is open to the eastward and westward, but is not well sheltered from the northward, the Mia-tao Islands being too distant to break off much of either wind or swell from that quarter. The anchoring-ground consists, in great part, of hard, sharp rocks; and at about a mile and a quarter from the shore is a dangerous reef, covered at high water, extending nearly a mile, east and west, round which the water shoals so suddenly as to render any approach to it very perilous. At Teng-chow-fu is constructed a kind of dock or basin for vessels to load or discharge their cargoes. The entrance into it is between two piers, and is from thirty to forty feet in width. The ground near the sea-coast is richly cultivated, and rises in a gentle ascent until terminated by high, broken, and barren mountains, apparently granitic. The rise and fall of the tides in the Strait of Mia-tao are about seven feet. The flood-tide runs *east*, towards the sea; the ebb runs to the *westward*, into the Gulf of Pekin."

This latter piece of information applies, perhaps, to the eddy tide in the anchorage off Teng-chow-fu, for when the Furious struck on an unknown sandbank in passing through these straits (at a later hour in the afternoon), we found the ebb-tide running, as it should do, out of the Gulf of Pecheli; and it will be hereafter shown that off the Peiho River the flood and ebb evidently, from their direction, run in and out of the gulf according to natural laws, the flood-tide coming from the sea.

We had a rattling breeze behind us, with every token of an increase, both in the appearance of the sky and fall of the barometer, and I knew that at this

season dense fogs might be expected, with an almost
unknown sea before me. There was no anchorage
east of Mia-tao Islands—the evening of April 13th
fast closing in—and consequently no time was to be
lost in pushing through the straits, so as to have sea-
room in the Gulf of Pecheli. I had been cautioned by
the Russian officers who visited this channel in 1857
not to trust the charts as to the limit of the extensive
shoal which runs out from the Shantung coast, and
projects in a N.W. direction, but to borrow freely upon
the right hand, as the islands of Chang-shan and Ta-
he-san were steep. Keeping this in mind, seeing quite
distinctly the sandspit which runs off from Chang-
shan, and observing a large fleet of junks ahead, as
well as others running the same way as ourselves, I
steered boldly through the strait, but suddenly struck
a sandbank almost as steep as a wall, which brought
the Furious up all standing, with her stem in 11 feet
water, her centre in 14 feet, and her afterpart in 5
fathoms. Of course we had gone ashore as a man-of-
war should do, according to printed instructions and
articles of war—leads going, anchors clear, masthead
man in his station, and the captain, master, and officer
of the watch on the paddle-boxes. With a little trouble
we were off in deep water again by 6.30 P.M., none the
worse for our feat; although our little friend the
Slaney, being in tow when we brought up thus suddenly,

ran into us and damaged herself somewhat. Had
time and circumstances admitted of it, we should have
waited until next day to examine this danger; it is
either a prolongation of the sandspit of the Mia-tao
Islands, or else a detached patch. I am inclined to
think the latter, as it is about three-quarters of a mile
from the extreme laid down in the charts.* And subsequent to this event, H.M.S. Samson, towing up two
gunboats, appears to have scraped so close to it that
the bight of the hawser, by which she had a gunboat
in tow, fouled it; and the gunboat Leven, running out
of the gulf in the same spot, suddenly shoaled her
water from several fathoms to 13 feet—the spit from
the island being at the time plainly visible.

To return to the Furious. The night was fine
though dark. Ta-he-shan, the nearest of the Mia-tao
Isles, was visible on the right hand, and beyond it
glimmered a perfect Oxford Street of lights from a
fleet of junks at anchor in the strait. Guided by these
vessels and our chart, going as slow as possible, we
pushed on, shaving sometimes unpleasantly close to the
wonder-struck junkmen of Shantung, many of whom,
perhaps, had only as yet heard of foreign steamers by
report, and now, for the first time, saw a huge appari-

---

* Position of H.M.S. Furious when aground:—East extreme of Long
Island (Chang-shan) just open of the south extreme, and the west ex
treme of Ta-he-san Island N.W. by W.

tion advancing against the tide, uttering strange noises, commanded in strange language, glaring from two huge eyes of red and green (the steam lights), and beating the waters like one of their own mythical dragons of the sea. No wonder they exclaimed, " Hi-yaw!" Thus threading our way, by eleven o'clock we had cleared the shoals of Teng-chow-fu, and shaped a course by midnight across the Gulf of Pecheli for the entrance of the river leading to Pekin.

Nothing could have been more charming than the climate in which we had revelled along that coast of Shantung, and the sight of hills and mountainous country was very refreshing to our plain-sickened eyes ; for it requires a Dutchman to appreciate that flat, rich, unctuous valley around Shanghai. The province of Shantung is, however, said to be only mountainous in its eastern half—the rest forms a part of the great plain of China—a plain which rolls south from Pekin, gradually extending in width until its huge base rests at a distance of 600 miles against the foot of the moun-tains of Chekeang and Kiangsi. Eastern Shantung, a mass of hill, mountain, plateau, and valley, larger than Ireland, appears, therefore, like an island which has been connected with China proper by the gradual silt-ing up of some ancient water-channel : just, for in-stance, what may occur to the Corean Peninsula itself, if, as reported, the erratic Hoang-ho should commence

to discharge its waters and alluvium into the Gulf of
Pecheli, and thus assuredly fill it up.

To the seaports of this Shantung promontory will
hereafter flock our ships; to Teng-chow-fu or some
other foo (city), those pioneers of civilisation and commerce, whom one can see looming in the future of Northern China, will retreat during the rigours of a Pekinese
winter. Its shores will be one day the watering-places
of the ambassadors, diplomatists, and their retainers,
whom duty or policy may oblige us to place stationary
within ear-shot of Emperor and court. It requires no
prescience to foresee the importance of this promontory
in the future of Northern China; and Teng-chow-fu,
unless I am very much mistaken, will, within ten years,
be to the north what Shanghai is to the centre, and
Canton to the south of this huge empire.

The Mia-tao Isles are a series of stepping-stones
across the entrance of the Gulf of Pecheli; they are
lofty and picturesque without being barren. There
are, of course, several channels through them, and
some ugly detached rocks or reefs; but the Strait of
Mia-tao, between Shantung and the westernmost
isle, is perfectly safe when it shall have been properly
surveyed, and affords an excellent anchorage or roadstead. A glance at a chart will show how the islands
to the north, the sandspit of Chang-shan to the east,
the coast of Shantung to the south, and the shoals of

Teng-chow-fu Point to the west, shield this roadstead
of Mia-tao on every side from the seas adjacent; whilst
vessels desirous of seeking a still quieter spot for discharging cargo and repairing damages, have but to
anchor between the islands of Mia-tao and Chang-shan.
The bottom throughout is mud, or mud and sand;
depths to be found at choice from seven to four fathoms. The islands are inhabited; fresh water is
abundant, and such supplies as may be needed, and
they do not afford, may be easily procured from Teng-
chow-fu, only five miles distant. If, as may be fully
anticipated, a few short years hence this anchorage be
much frequented by European shipping, it will be the
seaport, so to speak, of Teng-chow-fu, and a colony of
all those who live by, and live upon, the merchant,
shipmaster, and shipowner, will be rapidly formed on
the adjacent islands; and most assuredly, whenever it
is possible to do so, European settlements or commercial posts should in China be invariably formed on
such islands. They are easier protected from hostilities than similar posts on the mainland; and being
apart from the population of the Chinese hives, there
is much less risk of collision or misunderstanding with
mandarins, literati, or native custom-house officers.
The roadstead of Mia-tao is well known to most of
the junks trading with Northern China. In the course
of my researches at Shanghai, my attention was re-

peatedly called to it as the great rendezvous of the
native trade in that quarter; and I had sometimes
visions of suddenly swooping down upon the trade of
Northern China, and of applying that material pressure
to the Chinese intellect, which is so well understood by
them—a pressure which we call in the East moral
pressure! It was all a mere vision—a dream. It was
all very well for Sir Humphrey Davy to wish he was
born twenty-five years later; we sailors may only wish
we had been born half-a-century earlier. Lo, as I
have said, after having slain Chinamen at Canton—
scaled the city walls—eaten the sacred carp out of
ponds, each of which the horror-stricken Borzes believed at least to be a departed abbot—in short, done
all that was in our power to burn, sink, ravage, and
destroy around and in the city of Canton, we sailed,
or rather steamed, peaceably through a fleet of grain
vessels, especially sent to provision the capital of China,
and enable it to hold out against our demands! It is
a funny country China, and we all do funny things in
it. The Chinaman is not the only funny fellow there,
believe me.

There are, however, no birds in last year's nests—it
is useless now to mourn over lost opportunities. Returning, therefore, to my theme, the roadstead of Mia-
tao, I may say that it is from thence that the native
traders from the south take their departure afresh for

the ports of Manchuria (or Shingking), the Corea, and
Gulf of Leotong. Those bound to either of the two
former provinces steer north along the islands which
guard the entrance of the gulf, until they strike Cape
Lao-thie-shan (the extreme of a peninsula strangely
named in our maps the Regent's Sword) ; thence they
diverge on their respective coasting voyages ; whilst
the grain-junks bound to the Peiho River take advan
tage of a propitious breeze, and steer direct for it across
the Gulf of Pecheli from Mia-tao Strait.

Thither we must now follow the Furious, which,
through a muddy sea and murky atmosphere, which
sadly limited the circle of vision, staggered before a
freshening breeze, in never more than twelve fathoms
water, for the low and shallow coast of Chili. Know
ing how limited was our knowledge of this sea, how
scant the soundings, the set of currents, or existence
of shoals or rocks, one might have been serious or
anxious in thus plunging along at a speed of eight
knots per hour, had it not been that we were constantly sighting some queer-looking "argosy" of China,
rolling along like nothing else earthly but what she
was—"a junk at sea," and the feeling that a sea which
a Chinaman can navigate in such clumsy craft ought
to be, and is, child's play to an English seaman.

At noon on April 14th, we found by observations that the current had set the ship 2.2 miles

per hour to the south-west during the twelve hours we had been in the gulf, and we altered course accordingly. This southerly current we had subsequently reason to believe to be very frequent, if not constant, at this season of the year; for nearly all the vessels which made the traverse experienced it, in a more or less degree, until the end of May; and it is so far advantageous, that it will keep a ship clear of the Sha-liu-tien shoals, and of her approach to the coast of Chili the lead-line will give ample warning. The cause of such a current is very easily explainable. A prodigious discharge of water, occasioned by summer thaws, must, in March, April, May, and June, be thrown into the Gulfs of Leo-tung and Pecheli from the high lands and snow-covered plains of Mongolia and Manchuria. The surplus of what is not carried off by evaporation must flow southward into the Yellow Sea, naturally causing a constant current in that direction, only partially checked by the flood-tide.

From noon the soundings gradually decreased; many junks were seen on every hand, standing in the same way as ourselves; and just as we had run by patent log the distance from our position at noon, the land about the entrance of the Peiho rose like a black line out of the waters on the western horizon, and proved that the Admiralty chart was so far very correct.

Running into four fathoms water, and sighting the leading marks over the bar of the Peiho River—a bar which we did not *then* despair of carrying the Furious across—we shortened sail, and anchored close to the Russian war-steamer America, bearing the flag of the Admiral and Plenipotentiary Count Putiatin. Shortly afterwards, H.M.S. Pique, Captain Sir F. Nicolson, joined us.

It must be acknowledged that our anchorage, as well as the view of the adjacent coast, was far from cheering. We were eight and a half miles off the shore, with only twenty-two feet under our keel at low-water. The sea was of a thick muddy colour, the sky murky and misty. Very indistinctly visible to the westward the low land at the mouth of the Peiho was seen dancing from the effects of refraction, whilst three eminences, more marked in outline than the rest, denoted the position of the forts and batteries of Taku, which, of course, we well knew, in spite of the surf, the bar, and all the Tartars in Mongolia, would very shortly be ours.

At night the breeze slackened somewhat, and the sea became overspread with phosphoric light, as brilliant as any ever witnessed in equatorial regions; this, however, only took place once or twice, and that during the early period of our stay in the gulf. The waters of the gulf were at first almost as muddy in

appearance as those of the Yang-tse-kiang, but this
condition gradually abated as the season advanced, and
in July the water at the anchorage was simply of a
turbid sea-green colour. This change arises, probably,
from the rivers having ceased to throw so large a
volume into the Gulf of Pecheli after the snows of the
uplands had melted away, and because the constant
action of the southerly monsoon forces in more salt
water from the seas to the south.

The junkmen called our attention to the increase of
water occasioned by the presence of the monsoon into
such a *cul-de-sac* as the Gulf of Pecheli; and I estimated that when we left in July, there was then on an
average nearly a foot more water at our anchorage than
when we arrived in April. This phenomenon was,
however, by no means strange to me after my experiences in the Black Sea, and especially in the Sea of
Azov.

It has seldom been my fate to anchor in a more
dreary spot than that off the bar of the Peiho River,
or one more unpromising as a secure place for a ship;
but time reconciled us considerably to the apparent
deficiencies of the anchorage we were in, and I have
no hesitation in saying that, as a summer holding-
ground, it is sufficiently safe—that is, from April 14th
to the end of September. Vessels, we know, have
been much later at it; and in a steamer, with good

anchors and cables, the roadstead might be used until the winter ice, which forms in the rivers, compelled her to start for Mia-tao Strait. During the eleven weeks the Furious and squadron remained at the anchorage, smart double - reef topsail breezes were frequent, and sometimes very heavy squalls, in which the wind shifted abruptly, and blew equally hard from south-east to north-west or south-west to north. The sea that arose on these occasions was never trying to the ships, neither did any of them have to get down their topgallant-masts on account of the weather ; but for boat - work, intercommunication between vessels or with the shore, or to discharge the cargoes of mer-chantmen, there was often sufficient sea to render such operations hazardous, if not impossible. The heaviest sea experienced was from the south-east, the drift of the waves from that direction being the greatest. The north-east gales, which in the offing outside the Sha-liu-tien shoals make perhaps the heaviest sea experi-enced in the gulf, are broken where ships lie at anchor by those extensive sandbanks, of which a very good chart was published by the Admiralty, in the year 1840, compiled by Mr Nosworthy, of H.M.S. Pylades.

The south-west monsoon, except at spring tides, or rather on full and change of the moon, lulled during the night, and freshened during the afternoon, sometimes

blowing stiff when high-water occurred about 4 P.M.
The vessels being always to windward, and in the
wind's eye of the bar, added to the difficulties of
communication in open boats. When the gunboats
arrived, they of course relieved us of all anxiety on
that score, though the depth of water upon the bar
compelled that intercommunication with the shore to
be confined to certain times of tide.

All day long, junks were continually arriving from
the south and from the north. They usually accumulated outside the bar to await high-water, and then
they would scramble in in such huge squadrons, that
one only wondered how they managed to stow away
in what looked from our anchorage a mere thread of
water. The junks, or rather decked lighters, from the
north, were extraordinary looking crafts—not unlike
Dutch Doggerbank boats — and though small, they
evidently were cut out and rigged for heavy weather
and a broken sea. Not only were these vessels divided
into compartments like all other junks, but the hatch-
way of each compartment was singularly small, and
the combings were carried up some feet high in the
centre of the vessel, as well as further secured from
the wash of the sea by snug covers, and many lashings.
Beans, millet, and sesame-seed was their general cargo,
and we observed here that flax rope was often seen,
whilst wooden anchors were carefully eschewed, every

junk or boat having iron grapnels. Lord Elgin authorised the detention of a couple of these vessels, though
of course force was only so far used as to compel the
owners to hire their craft. Our seamen, with their usual
drollery, christened these two ships of Shinking, the
Bean and Sweet-Pea, their cargoes consisting of pulse,
resembling those so well known to our men ; and
H.M. ships Bean and Pease did good service, whilst we
were waiting for all the forces to arrive, without
which Lord Elgin's presence off the entrance of the
Peiho River was of as much use as if he and the
Furious had been a constellation in the heavens
above it. I first of all established a tide-pole and
registry on board the ship, and then placed another
upon the bar, to obtain with certainty the depth of
water upon that bar, and the actual rise and fall of
tide, as well as the time of high-water at full and
change — three most essential points, upon all of
which there was as yet great ignorance or uncer-
tainty. For instance, Horsburgh's Directory gave
the time of high-water at full and change as at
3h. 30m. The Admiralty Chart (No. 1391) of
1840, said it was at 2h. 45m. ; and the Russian
officers assured me both were wrong, for they believed it to be at about 4 P.M. This serious discre-
pancy, the general reader will understand to involve
the question of the hour at which the bar of the Peiho

River was passable for vessels intending to communicate with or attack the fortifications of Taku. The tide-table, excellently kept by my gallant and zealous lieutenants, and arranged by that best of masters, Stephen Court, is annexed, and reflects no small credit upon their united zeal and industry. Living, as I and several of my men and officers did, in our boats upon this bar during the first week or ten days, and viewing the preparations of the Chinese then made, in their normal condition, it will be as well to give them. On the port or left hand of the entrance of the river, there were three works, known as the South, Middle, and North Forts. The South Fort was 150 yards in frontage; it mounted ten guns, apparently brass ones; the parapet was very slight, and the work open to the rear; on its outer flank there was a small outwork mounting four guns, as if to sweep the face on the beach. The Middle Fort had a front of equal extent, and likewise mounted ten guns. Large bodies of men were constantly at work connecting these two works by a parapet and covered way. But the Middle Fort was already connected with the North Fort by a long battery in which the guns were almost *en barbet*. We counted sixteen guns in this battery. The North Fort mounted ten or twelve guns, some of them of very heavy calibre. In short, there were 49 guns in position on the left hand batteries, and a force of

about 4000 men fell in for parade under our eyes on
the 16th April ; and I may add, because any information may be useful, that there was a flag to at least
every four men. Napier's simile of the Belooch army,
being gorgeous as a field of " poppies," would have
been no exaggeration, if applied to the calico army
which had been sent to repel us, the vain conquerors
of the city of Canton.   My first feeling was one of in-
dignation, that we, the finest navy in the world, as well
as the representatives of the army of France, could
only succeed in frightening the Chinese sufficiently to
make them send such a force and such a quantity of
flags, to strike terror to our souls. The fort on the
right bank was a bit of a breast - work thrown up
to seaward of an ancient castle, which had stood there
from almost time immemorial. We could not at first
make out that there were any guns in it, but were
not certain. The position of these forts, in a defensive point of view, was excellent, and it only required
time and science to make them extremely ugly places
to attack.

The Peiho River, which, being translated, means
" the North River," has its sources in the high lands
at no great distance beyond Pekin, and runs for the
major portion of its tortuous course through a level
country, the velocity of its stream, rather than the
volume of its water, having scoured out a narrow bed

in the stiff clay which forms the substratum of the
plain of Chili.   This scouring force, however, as in all
other streams, becomes weakened as it approaches the
sea, owing to the low level of the shores allowing a
constant overflow, and instead of cutting a twelve-feet
channel straight out into the Gulf of Pecheli, the
depth of the river suddenly decreases, and the river
discharges itself over an area several miles in extent,
forming what is known as the Bar.

The best, indeed the only, chart we possessed of this
bar of the Peiho River is the American one, and I can
testify to its general correctness, except that the water
found by the Americans on the bar was nearly two
feet deeper at low-water than it is at present — an
error probably caused from computation, instead of
doing as we did, remaining constantly upon the bar
from high-water to dead low-water.

The manner in which that American chart came
into my possession, and afterwards into general use
throughout the squadron, is a proof of the necessity
for a better understanding between geographers of
different countries, and a more frequent interchange of
information collected by each.   I will state the circumstances to exemplify the case :—Prior to leaving
Hong-Kong in March 1858, a conviction that the
ultimate result of our Canton operations would be
to carry the Furious and the British ambassador

to the Peiho River, induced me to seek carefully
for any information bearing upon that part of China.
I soon found that in the British chart-boxes there was
nothing about the Peiho beyond the fact that the Hon.
Company's steamer Madagascar had once crossed the
bar, but there was no certainty as to what water she
carried over it. The French, of course, were equally
ignorant; but from Mr Reed, the American ambassador, as well as Captain Du Pont of the U.S. frigate
Minnesota, I learned that, much to their astonishment,
Count Putiatin, the Russian envoy, had shown them
an *American survey* of the bar of the Peiho River,
made by the officers of the United States ship John
Hancock, of which they had been previously ignorant,
and of which no copy had even been supplied them
from the Hydrographic Bureau at Washington. That
it was authentic, however, there could be no doubt,
and the good folks of the United States can best explain how it was that a Russian could procure a copy
of an official record before it was furnished to their
own accredited minister. Count Putiatin made no
secret of his valuable document, and when we arrived
at Shanghai, and found him there, he very kindly
allowed me to make a copy of it, and added some
kind and valuable information touching the tides off
the Peiho and the dangers in Mia-tao Strait. Directly
the Pique joined the Furious off the Peiho River, I

was able to lend her Captain the American chart to
copy, and we subsequently did as much for the flag-
ship.

The bar of the Peiho River, measured on the seaward side, extends in a great curve of six miles in
length, and at its narrowest point between the deep
water within and without, it is two miles wide. It
consists of very stiff clay, with a few patches of shingle
here and there ; the whole overlaid by nine or ten
inches of earthy deposit from the river. At low-water
spring-tides we only found two feet water upon the bar
in the deepest places ; indeed, on more than one occasion whilst living upon it in boats, we found that a
stiff breeze off-shore reduced the water to only a foot
in depth. The deepest water observed in calm weather,
when such observations could be relied upon, showed a
depth of rather more than eleven feet at high-water
of spring-tide. These observations agreed admirably
with that observed on board H.M.S. Furious—viz.,
H.W. at F. & C. of ☾ 4h. 8m., and rise and fall =
nine English feet. It is, however, possible that in the
Gulf of Pecheli, as in other shallow, land-locked seas,
these data are to some degree dependent upon the season of the year ; and that winds of a certain force or
from certain directions may at other seasons retard or
hasten the time of high-water, and affect the height of
water upon the bar to the extent of a foot or eighteen

inches. At any rate, it is certain that vessels drawing
ten feet eight inches can easily cross the bar of the
Peiho at spring-tides; and on interrogating the masters
of trading junks, through my friend Mr Lay, I learned
that the largest vessels trading with Tientsin varied
from 300 to 500 tons burden, but never exceeded
eleven English feet in draught. The Chinese mark the
channel over the bar with bamboos; their positions
when we arrived were inserted in the chart, but, as
they subsequently cut some of these bamboos away, we
replaced them with buoys, by means of which the gunboats and despatch-vessels of the allied squadron were
eventually carried safely over the bar into the Peiho
River on May 19, 1858.

There is no continuous surf upon the bar; but when
it blows a fresh breeze from the south-east there is
quite enough sea on to render the bar highly dangerous
for open boats; indeed, the smallest native craft used
in this neighbourhood are decked. My own impression
is that when the Pekinese Government grows wiser it
will be very easy to cut a channel through the bar, and
that, by driving a few piles along its margin to confine
the force of the current in the same direction, a passage
for junks will be made fit for all times of tide. The
force of the current of the Peiho River at its mouth is
always much affected by the direction of the wind; in
calms it runs from two to two and a half knots per

hour. During the first three hours of the flood and the last three of the ebb tide, the current sets directly in and out over the bar, through its gutter-like channel ; but directly that the tide is high enough to cover the mud-flats, the direction of the current follows that of the tides in the offing—the flood going northerly, the ebb southerly.

Directly the bar is crossed a deep channel is entered, which, although tortuous, has never less than twelve feet water in it at high-water, and in many places much more, all the way from the entrance to Tientsin. Off some of the salient points where the river takes a sharp turn, projecting spits of mud or sand are sometimes found ; but the general character was uniform—namely, a muddy stream running through flat country, wonderfully free from all obstructions, and the channel generally steep to the river bank. There are strong indications of vernal and autumnal inundations during the ascent of the first fifteen miles from the sea ; but beyond that distance the river banks as far as Tientsin were nowhere artificial, but rose with a natural abrupt escarp three to six feet above high-water mark. It would be difficult to account for the sharp bends in this river or its generally tortuous course, seeing that it runs through a plain as level as a table, and has had apparently only to cut its way through stiff blue or yellow clay ; nevertheless, in the short distance of thirty miles which intervenes between the city of Tientsin and Taku, at its mouth, the river turns and twists over not less than fifty miles of ground, very much as laid down in the map accompanying the account of Lord Macartney's embassy to Taku in 1793—that map, however, is decidedly very incorrect directly Tientsin is passed.

Of the combat of the 20th May 1858, in which the works of Taku fell so easily into our hands, I need not speak; the resistance was so trifling that few would be inclined to claim much honour in that affair. I shall not dwell upon it, farther than to express my conviction that the garrisons of those forts were not sufficiently punished to impress them with a due sense of the penalty of opposing Europeans. Humanity may have had weight with us; but with those who misunderstand forbearance, humanity is, in my opinion, a weakness. Those unscathed garrisons of 1858 have since returned to slay hundreds of our countrymen in an ambuscade, and mistaken forbearance will cost us hundreds of lives and millions of money in 1860. Let us be wiser for the future.

The capture of the earthworks effected and all the brass guns shipped off as trophies, the forces embarked in the ever-zealous gunboats, and advanced up the Peiho at a leisurely rate. It was our good fortune in the boats of the Furious to be detailed

to the Bustard, commanded by Lieutenant Hallowes.
Six boats and a hundred men thrown upon the comforts and hospitality of a tiny gunboat, were enough
to tax the good-nature of those belonging to her ;
but I am sure all my officers and men would bear me
out in saying that that good-nature of the Bustard's
fully stood the severe test, and that we all shall long
remember the kindness experienced.   The weather was
already sultry, and occasionally distressingly so.   Even
in May, hot, dry winds came on, in which the slightest
exertion was disagreeably trying.   We used quinine
freely; in fact, each man of my crew had a dram of
quinine wine regularly every morning during the whole
time we were in the river, and we had not a single case
of fever in consequence ; but it must be remembered
that we had little, if any, labour or exertion.   The
gunboats towed us everywhere ; awnings constantly
screened us from the sun, food was very plentiful and
in great variety, the men in the highest spirits, and
we never had a wet jacket on our backs, or a wet plank
to sleep upon, during the whole time we were in the
Peiho River.

Apart from the natural excitement of breaking in
on new ground as belligerents, nothing could be less
interesting than the first part of the ascent of the Peiho
River.   On either hand extended a dreary mud flat,
which looked as if it had been only yesterday wrung

from the sea. Reeds, rushes, and such plants as love a
marshy or saline soil, were seen in patches ; but the
major portion was nought but a saline, the glistening
product of which, piled in great pyramids by the thrifty
Chinese, broke the uniformity of the scenery. The
banks of the river were, however, turned to every possible advantage by a swarming population. Mud-built
villages commenced within a mile of the entrance : the
largest of them, "Taku," has had one visit from us, which
its unfortunate but strong-smelling inhabitants will long
have occasion to remember.* Wretched, dirty, and foul-
smelling though these villages appeared to the eye of an
European, they were, in fact, exceeding rich with the
hoarded fruits of commercial and agricultural industry ;
and the plunder carried off from Taku, which looked
about as wretched as an English fishing-village in the
winter time, could not have been found by the most
experienced leader of a " razzia " in anything smaller
than one of our large cities. In front of each of these
villages fleets of junks were anchored or hauled into
mud docks cut in the banks ; the majority were grain-
vessels or vessels pressed into that service by our active
friend the Taoutae of Shanghai, who remorselessly applies to his master's service the shipping of Amoy, Fu-

* I need hardly say that it will be long remembered for the
heroic fight of Admiral Hope's forces, when caught in an ambuscade,
June 1859.

chow-fu, Shanghai, or Shantung, paying them only a small nominal freight—an act of oppression against which, instead of murmuring, the Chinese shipmaster quietly indemnifies himself by carrying a contraband venture of European produce, opium, cottons, hardware, gimcrack, and lucifer matches, &c., which he charges an enormous price upon, and cheats the Government of all taxes and dues.

The Peiho improved rapidly as we ascended it ; the soil overlying the clay stratum increased in depth and fertility, signs of agriculture multiplied on either hand, fields of Indian corn, millet, bearded wheat, lettuces, and radishes, followed in rapid succession. The villages were embosomed in fruit orchards, or hid their ugliness in groves of handsome trees. Some of the reaches of the river became exceedingly picturesque, although there was a lack of the grotesque temple and quaint pagoda which give so marked a character to Chinese scenery in the south. From the masthead of the gunboat I was in, the villages, population, and cultivation appeared confined to the immediate vicinity of the Peiho, forming two belts, varying from two to four miles in width. This I could only account for by the want of water elsewhere, and it was remarkable that in a distance of fifty miles we only counted two small streams or creeks flowing into the Peiho. Beyond this belt of cultivation and its teeming popula-

tion a wide steppe was seen extending, on which
trees were scarce and the houses few and isolated. It
put me much in mind of the interminable plains of
Russia: however, I do not mean to assert that the
plain of Chili is uninhabited, but that it is so by com-
parison with the borders of the fresh-water streams, of
which there are several flowing into the sea besides the
Peiho, if the Chinese are to be believed. I counted at
one time no less than twenty-five villages in sight from
the masthead, and often ten or fifteen were visible: they
were none of them ruined in condition, and all appeared
full of inhabitants—stalwart naked labourers and hosts
of noisy healthy children; women were not seen until
afterwards, but of them there was no lack. Our first
arrival, gunboats and Europeans, was a startling event
to these poor villagers; but a stranger sight for us,
was to see the whole male population of a village
ranged along the bank, on their hands and knees, and
performing " kotow " as our gunboats passed. Besides
this form of respect and fear for the Fanqui, they
each offered a token of peace and amity in the shape
of a fowl, and here and there some, more frightened
than the rest, shouted to the interpreter, Mr H. N.
Lay, " Hail, great king! Oh, pray be pleased to dis-
embark and reign over us!" One man at a village,
who, I fancy, was a Christian convert, improved upon
the proceedings by placing himself on his knees in the

position of adoration, and continued so long as H.M. gunboat Bustard remained in sight. He, poor fellow, was no doubt anxious to propitiate the demon that had so suddenly burst upon the quietude of his Chinese village; but the application of his Christian teaching was as original as that of some Sandwich Islanders, whom I heard not many years ago singing the 64th Psalm to soothe the heathen goddess who, they believe, presides over their troublesome volcano.

At a point about four miles below Tientsin, the river makes a most extraordinary series of curves and twists, and here, had they had more time given, it was evident that the authorities intended to make another stand. An extensive intrenched camp was just being constructed in an admirable position, and a battery was outlined which would have effectually swept the reach. The junks were packed so close in this reach that we had some difficulty in screwing our way through them; and I could not help thinking that if the Chinese or Tartars had had all the patriotism some people suppose, they might easily have destroyed us, by simply setting their vessels on fire. It was not so, however. The Imperial forces could just be seen encamped under some trees about 3000 yards off; we potted at them with the bow-gun just to evince our good-will; and then, aided by the junkmen and inhabitants of the neighbouring houses, hastened the

native craft out of our way, and pulled out of the
stream a number of trees which had been thrown in
as the commencement of a barrier. Sir Frederick
Nicolson landed, and found some very rusty old guns
secreted in a brick kiln; they were, of course, dis-
abled. But it appeared as if all their new guns had
fallen into our hands at Taku, although we still heard
from the natives of some great fortifications up the
river, at or near Tung-chow, the highest point to
which the Peiho River is navigable.

A reach, three miles long in a straight line, brought
us in sight of the city of Tientsin, and the salt-heaps
or magazines, for which the city is famous, commence
at the end of this reach, near the remains of an old
ruined tower which once guarded the approach.
Owing to our consort, the Staunch, having grounded
in this said reach in trying to turn under steam, it
fell to the lot of the gunboat Bustard and Lieutenant-
Commander Hallowes to be the first vessel to steam
into the city of Tientsin. The interest of that forenoon's
work, May 26, 1858, will not be easily effaced from my
memory. As every fresh point mentioned by Barrow
and Ellis came in sight, I could not but recall with some
degree of elation the altered circumstances under which
the British flag now made its appearance. Then over the
craft bearing our ambassador floated a flag on which
was written the lie that he was bearing tribute to a

D

Chinese Emperor; mandarins and rabble indulged in all their impertinences and arrogance; and whereas then his audience with the Emperor took place to the air of "subjugation perfected!" played by a Pekin band, it now appeared more than probable that an English one would shortly be performing "God save the Queen!" in the same spot. As our tiny craft with her crew of seamen and marines from the Furious sped on, we came abreast of the huge pyramids of salt, 100 feet high and 200 feet long, which formed a magnificent defence, and we naturally hoped to see a gun appear in sight to add some *eclat* to our capture of Tientsin. But we looked in vain; not an armed man was visible anywhere. We now passed into the southern suburbs of the city—a long row of dingy hovels, the one on the eastern shore being the most extensive—or rather I ought to have said we screwed in between two long rows of human beings, piled head above head as thick as standing room would admit. Astonishment, wonder, and curiosity had mastered all their fears. Presently we saw a bridge of boats extending across ahead, and beyond it the river made a sharp bend to the right, whilst on the left the mouth of the Great Canal was distinctly visible. We all cheered with delight; we felt Tientsin was ours, and that in it we held, to use the figurative language of Shanghai, the throat of China! Although the mob officiously opened the bridge and appeared anxious to cheer us onward, I felt it was my duty to take up a position for commanding the southern face of the city walls, and as they were now only a few hundred yards off, we anchored at the bridge. Two conspicuous public buildings were visible from the Bustard; one ahead looked down the reach, which from its importance we supposed to be the temple at which, in 1793, Lord Macartney was met by the Emperor's legate. This building subsequently became the abode of the allied ambassadors. The other was only seen from the mast-head : it was a handsome isolated building on the plain, about 1200 yards distance from the river ; its gorgeous painting attracted our attention, and it strangely enough was the place in which the treaty of Tientsin was eventually signed. It was named by the Chinese " the Temple of the Glory of the Ocean."

Hardly had our anchor reached the bottom before Chinamen and boys began to swim off with fowls, eggs, fruits, and vegetables for sale; and as our seamen were revelling in a degree of wealth which was parti-cularly irksome to them, consisting of copper coin cap-tured in the batteries of Taku, the good folk of Tientsin were not a little astonished at the wonderful amount of wealth thus strangely pouring in upon them, and evinced every anxiety to take all possible advantage of

it. In the height of the excitement, which our men
increased to fever heat by showering handfuls of cash
among the crowd for a scramble, a midshipman stationed
aloft reported that a large body of Chinese troops were
quitting the Temple of the Glory of the Ocean and
marching into the city. The pivot-gun was rapidly
cleared away and pointed over the crowd : the buyers
and sellers became sadly agitated between fear and
cupidity. We made signs that all we required was
room enough to fire at their countrymen; they appreciated the joke amazingly, cleared a space of fifty yards
wide in front of the gun's muzzle, and then sat down
to see the fun. Happily for the retreating soldiery, as
well as for the Temple of the Glory of the Ocean, the
Bustard's gun could not be sufficiently elevated to clear
the adjacent housetops, and I was unwilling to fire
through them at the mandarins without some provoca-
tion, otherwise it is possible that His Excellency Lord
Elgin would not have found that said temple sufficiently
wind and water-tight for those conferences, which have
eventually led to the signature of the treaty of Tientsin
within its walls.

Having sent the boats of the Furious into the
Great Canal, under my gallant first lieutenant, Philip
Brock, to be able to say that my ship's boats had been
the first European ones to reach the northern end
of that remarkable work—a piece of vanity for which

I hope to be pardoned—I returned in my galley to meet the Coromandel, bearing the flag of the Commander - in - Chief, who joined us an hour or two afterwards.

Tientsin consists of a small walled city, built in the form of a square, each wall as nearly as possible a mile long, and each facing to the four cardinal points of the compass. In the centre of the four time-worn walls a single gate opens out, giving only four outlets, a pretty good proof that it is not a very large place, and has not a very numerous population. It stands at the angle formed between the south bank of the Great Canal and the river Peiho, but its walls are from two to three hundred yards from the water's edge. Suburbs of some extent lie to the north and west and east, but on the plain facing the southern wall, few, if any, houses are seen. These suburbs consist for the major part, as does the city, of mud-built houses, giving the whole place an appearance of meanness and poverty, little in keeping with the general reputation of Tientsin for wealth and commercial importance. Previous travellers have, they say, been always struck with the numbers and busy character of its population; we were disappointed in both respects, but it is possible that the circumstances under which we visited it may account for the seeming inactivity of the people ashore and afloat. The population did not appear to exceed

100,000 souls, yet the residents vowed that there were half a million souls in Tientsin. All the prodigious floating population spoken of by former embassies had naturally fled in their boats, and, moreover, it is quite possible that Tientsin, like Nijni-Novgorod, or other great marts of Russia and Siberia, becomes at times densely populated with merchants, boatmen, and other frequenters of fairs, and again relapses into what we saw it—a dull, dirty town, with no large fixed population, and not exhibiting (because it does not retain) any of the wealth which is constantly passing through it.

The streets within the city ran for the most part at right angles to each other; in the suburbs they were far more eccentric: all were excessively ill-kept, and of all the strong-smelling places it has been my hard fate to visit in this land of strong and foul smells, Tientsin city and suburbs—streets, houses, and inhabitants— are the most disagreeable. They seem to be aware of it, and perhaps feed largely upon garlic to master the difficulty; but to a visitor the odour is perfectly capable of giving one nosè-ache. The water drunk by the inhabitants is either that of the river or canal, and all day long thousands of stalwart water-bearers are rushing in and out of the city on four paved causeways especially intended for that purpose. This water, as it is drawn, is full of foreign matter and muddy:

the Chinese clear it by putting into it a very small
quantity of alum—a practice we found it necessary to
imitate, as the river water, in its natural state, gave
our men diarrhœa. The imperial salt stores lie on the
eastern bank of the river Peiho, and extend over a very
considerable area. The salt is piled in huge stacks or
pyramids, and carefully covered with matting. It is
sold to the dealers in bags of about 3 cwt., and forms
an important article of the imperial revenue in this
province. The supply of these stores is not confined to
the products of the vast salines around Taku, for we
learnt that much salt came from places to seaward, pro-.
bably the coasts of Shantung and Chili, and that up
the When-ho, or Salt River, there were either salines, or
brine pits, whence much of this necessary of life was procured. Next to these vast stores of salt which lined the
river banks, the wood stores of Tientsin appeared very
important and valuable. Acres of ground were covered
with magnificent slabs of beech-wood, most of them
100 feet long, and from 4 to 9 inches thick. This
wood enters largely into the construction of river
craft in the province, and, in spite of its tendency to
sun-rents, when coated with Chinese varnish, and
wetted twice or thrice a-day with water, stands the
powerful sun of Northern China remarkably well.
Nearly every house in the suburbs was a shop: those
to which we gained admittance were very well furnished

with the products of different parts of China; articles
from the southern and west provinces—Yunnan, Quan-
tung, and Fokien, &c.—being dear, showing the want
of greater facilities of interchange. Other articles—
such as rattans, canes, peppers, spices, sugar, &c.—
were plentiful; but they, as well as tea, were in great
demand, and dear. The profits that would have accrued to importers of all these articles would have been
very handsome, and I heard that it would have taken
many cargoes to have glutted the market. People at
home often suppose tea and sugar to be produced all
over China; but as a proof how great must be the
demand for sugar alone in Northern China, I would
point out from the Custom-house records of Shanghai, the following interesting figures, showing not
only the extraordinary vitality of commerce in China,
but the wonderful demand for tropical products in
the north :—

EUROPEAN IMPORTS.—Sugars Imported into Shanghai from Southern China and
the Straits of Malacca.

	Sugar Imported. Piculs.	Tons.	Value £ Sterling.
1855. None imported by European vessels	..	..	..
1856. During the entire year ending June 30th . . .	438,004 =	27,395 =	404,534
1857. During an entire year .	529,009 =	33,062 =	751,103
Increase in two years, . . .		5,667 =	346,569

And as a proof that there seems no limit to this expan-
sion, I have, whilst writing, received the Custom-house
returns, drawn up at Shanghai by my friend Mr

H. N. Lay, in which I find that during the year 1859
the imports of sugar had further increased to the wonderful amount of 53,452 tons, valued by the importers
at £1,078,743 sterling. In short, the sugar trade had
doubled itself in three years.

I do not deny that it is possible that a portion of this
used formerly to be imported in native craft, and that
it may only be considered as so much tonnage added
to the European carrying trade ; still it is said that the
native vessels visiting Shanghai have in no wise decreased in number in an equal ratio, which would have
been the case had the trade been merely one of transfer
from native to foreign bottoms. Nearly every shop I entered at Tientsin had some article or other of European
manufacture ; sad trash for the most part, but still high-
priced ; indeed I saw more British, American, and Ger-
man articles in Tientsin than the shops of Canton or
Shanghai usually exhibited. There being no staple
export from Tientsin, the trade there must be, to a very
great extent, an import one ; but from the profusion of
metals we observed here, there could be no difficulty as
to purchasing until some products, such as wool, hides,
tallow, and coals, were brought into the market as a
return. All the thousands of junks from the south
were leaving in ballast. This might have arisen from
the haste with which our unexpected arrival compelled
them to put to sea ; but I was told that, under all cir-

cumstances, they exported a great quantity of copper coin, or cash, as we call the Chinese currency, as well as some silver and gold.   Considering how severely China drains our money-market, we shall have every reason to rejoice if, apart from opium, we can discover some mode of creating a purely import trade in Northern China to balance the exports of the south.

Grain is, and must be, the great article of commerce in Tientsin.   Formerly, whilst China was at peace within its borders, the canal perfect, and communication between her rice-producing districts and the capital assured, it would have been difficult to have competed with our Indian rice against the Chinese farmer, but not impossible, for be it remembered we import that grain largely into Canton.   Rice from our Indian possessions, as well as from Siam and Java, mostly imported in European bottoms, is largely bought up at Shanghai and sent by junks to Tientsin.   Our great object should be, to be the carriers and feeders of the capital, and to deliver the food at Tientsin itself. Policy will then render the Court less likely to quarrel with us.   That the yearly imports of rice from abroad are on the increase in Northern China, there can be no doubt, when we see in the Custom-house returns for Shanghai the following figures :*—

* I have, in a subsequent chapter, dwelt more at length upon this subject, but introduce this paragraph as a record made upon the spot.

	Rice imported. Piculs.	Value in Teals.	Tons.	Value at Shanghai. £ sterling.
Year ⎰ Half year to June 30th, 1856 ⎱ Half year to Dec. 51st,	.. 110,000 =	.. 220,000 =	.. 7,000 =	.. 7,333
1857 ⎰ 1st half year, ⎱ 2d half year,	864,637 =	1,810,849 =	54,039 =	603,281
Increase in one year,			47,039 =	595,948

And how dire must be the need in Northern China for rice, is best proved by the following facts, which will give some assurance to the trader of the amount of fair profit he may count upon :—

			Dollars.	D.
Summer of 1858,	⎰ Rice at Shanghai,	=	3 a picul or	2 per lb.
	⎱ Rice at Tientsin,	=	6 ,,	4 ,,
Winter of 1857-1858,	Rice at Pekin,	=	12 ,,	8 ,,

Twelve dollars a picul for rice at Pekin was, of course, a starvation price to the masses ; and, indeed, judging by appearances, half that sum was equally so at Tientsin to the labouring classes.

Squalor, hunger, and misery seemed the general condition of the lower orders in this emporium of Northern China. I was much struck with the contrast in the appearance of the Chinese in and around Tientsin, and those I had been accustomed to see around our flourishing settlements in the south. There, they were fat and saucy; here, starving and subdued. There, contact with the much-contemned "barbarian" trader gave them food and raiment, and enabled them to be independent of mandarins and *squeezes*. Here, John Chinaman was in possession of all the rights, privileges, and advantages of his precious Government, and its laws in all their pristine purity ; and a pleasant privilege it must have been, judging by his appearance, and his love for Emperor and country. The exclamation of one of my boat's crew struck me as typifying, in strong vernacular, the condition of these people. He overheard a native giving information to one of our interpreters connected with the forces assembling between us and the capital ; and, shocked at the treachery, he exclaimed to his mate— "What a beggar, mate ! I'm blest if these chaps wouldn't sell their mothers, much less king and country !" and that is about the amount of morality and patriotism we found in Tientsin.

Apart from rice, the want of which affected the English force but little, I cannot say that we found a deficiency of food; and the merchants of Tientsin, who were held responsible by the authorities for our wants being properly satisfied, fulfilled their task very well ; sheep, poultry, vegetables, and fruit were procurable to any extent. We ordered beef, and cattle came ; there were occasional laments, on the part of the authorities, at our voracious consumption of an animal so useful for agricultural purposes, but there was no lack of them. The following tariff was laid down by the allied Commanders-in-Chief, in concurrence with the magistrates, as fair market prices ; and, according to our ideas of money, everything was very cheap.

TARIFF of PRICES established at Tientsin, 28th May 1858.

Bullocks (average 4 cwt.),........................10 dollars = 40s. each.
Sheep, ... 2 dollars = 8s. ,,
Fowls (per dozen), ... 1 dollar = 4s.
Ducks,.. 2 dollars = 8s. each.
Geese,... 2 dollars = 8s. ,,
Eggs (per 1000), ... 3 dollars = 12s.
Vegetables (per picul = cwt.),..........1 dollar 50 cts. = 6s.
Ice (per cwt.), ... 200 cash = 2d.
Pigs, according to size,...........From 1 dollar 50 cts. = 6s. each.
Yams (per cwt.),.................................... 1 dollar = 4s.
Pears and apples per (100),..................... 1 dollar = 4s.

It is but right, however, to remind those about to proceed again to Tientsin, that in procuring all these supplies we had the good-will and assistance of the authorities; and that those prices will be found somewhat low when we again attempt to procure food in spite of Imperial edicts and mandarin hostility.

The Peiho River, as will be seen by reference to the enclosed eye-sketch of Tientsin, turns sharply off to the right (or to the east) just at the junction of the Great Canal, and then recurves back for a mile to the westward before the channel again resumes its northerly and southerly direction. By this strange twist the river gives a vast increase of water frontage to the city and suburbs. Immediately opposite to the salient point formed by this sudden bend, a small canal is seen on the eastern shore, and numbers of small boats, of a peculiarly flat construction, came daily down it laden with grain and millet-seed, and then

ascended the Peiho and When-ho Rivers. I believe they came from the city of Lutai, situated on a
stream northward of the Peiho, flowing nearly parallel
to the lower portion of its course, in discharging itself
into the sea about ten miles north-east of the entrance
of the Peiho. This stream we had early information
about, and the junk-sailors said it was largely used as a
place of import for vessels of lighter draught than those
usually ascending the Peiho as high as Tientsin, and
that a canal from Lutai enabled boats to convey the cargoes to Tientsin and Pekin. After warlike operations
commenced, and trade was totally interrupted in the
Peiho, this northern stream was largely used by the
Chinese, and fleets of junks varying from 25 to 50 in
number were constantly counted from the Furious going in and out of it. For some reason or other none
of the British vessels visited it, but in any future operations against Pekin the blockade of this stream will
be as necessary as that of the Peiho.

To return to the Peiho. Abreast the town—indeed,
throughout the whole extent of Tientsin—there was at
least eighteen feet at low-water, without a single shoal
or obstruction ; but just as the northern suburb is
cleared, an extensive shallow commences, a mile in extent, having only six feet on it at low-water, and about
ten feet at high-water. Just above this flat, a fine
canal is seen to the north-west, spanned by a handsome

bridge; this canal, we were informed, communicated
with the great city of "Pan-ching" or "Pan-ting."
Vast numbers of river-craft were reported to have
escaped up this artificial stream. In Macartney's map
this canal is not marked, or perhaps it has been subsequently constructed, although of that I have strong
doubts. The river beyond the canal, and just at the
confluence of the When-ho, or Salt River, deepens
suddenly to five fathoms, but does not long remain so,
as the Peiho now commences to assume a totally different character to what it is below Tientsin. Artificial
embankments exist on either side of the Peiho River,
directly the mouth of the When-ho is passed, especially
on the eastern hand, and, apart from shallows, the
channel is very narrow, and very tortuous. We soon
found it necessary to abandon the Bustard gunboat
for one of lighter draught, the Kestrel, Lieutenant
Rason in command. Taking advantage of high-water,
which only gave us from six to seven feet in the deepest
part of a long reach, three miles above the When-ho,
we pushed past several populous villages, the men and
boys in which voluntarily turned out to track our
boats, or drag at the gunboat's hawsers. The river
was nowhere more than one hundred yards broad, in
many places not more than two hundred feet, and the
difficulties of navigation increased apace as we advanced.
Under these circumstances, the senior officer decided

on not risking the grounding of the gunboat where she would not float off until the next spring-tides; we therefore turned back into our reconnaissance when abreast of the village named, I believe, "Quam-yin," and about nine to ten miles beyond Tientsin. At this point there was still a rise of tide of two feet six inches, and the flood was perceptible. The river was two hundred feet broad, with a narrow channel, in which from eight to ten feet water existed for a width of twenty-five feet, equal to about that of a gunboat; the rest of the stream was very shoal. Three fine villages were in sight, the farthest, a brick-built one, of evident importance.*

There was every appearance, in marks upon the river bank, of the river being at times much higher than when we saw it, and, from all I heard, I feel little doubt that, in early spring during the thaws, and in autumn or summer rains, there would be no difficulty in one of our small-class gunboats, lightened to four feet, ascending *one-third* of the way up to Tung-chow, the landing-place for the city of Pekin, or about twenty miles above Tientsin, leaving only forty miles to be done with rowboats. A boatman of the Pehio, whom I interrogated through Mr Lay, said that one-third of the way between Tientsin and Tung-chow, the river had deep water in it; that in the next third it was as

---

* The proximity of the villages to the river bank is a strong argument against inundations being frequent.

deep as up to his waist, and the rest of the way it was
only knee-deep. It is true that, during the time the
water in the Peiho is highest, the current would be
strongest; still that would be no great obstacle with
steam-power, and an unlimited amount of manual
labour at command. The country above Tientsin
varied in no degree from that immediately below it.
A splendid paved road exists between Tientsin and
Pekin, and in dry weather the whole plain is passable
for carriages, men, or horses. If, at any future time,
military operations against Pekin be necessary, the
months of April, May, and June would be the best to
employ. The course of the Peiho should be followed
to Tung-chow for facilities of transport, supplies,
manual labour, and fresh-water; depôts should be there
established, and the fall of Pekin would be assured
with no great difficulty.

The arrival of the imperial emissaries, Kweiliang
and Hwashana, put a stop to all our military and
naval explorations. Humanity forbids a Christian nation to prosecute war after a foe had sued for peace,
yet I was not singular in the feeling that the imperial government had not been sufficiently thrashed
to make a lasting impression upon their minds, or
to give us a lasting treaty. The skill with which
Lord Elgin succeeded, during that month of negotiations, in threatening a resumption of warlike ope-

E

rations, directly his arguments failed, and masking
our real weakness, was very great; and he had, at
the same time, to counterfoil the policy of the Russians and Americans, both of whom, strange to say,
proved to be by no means anxious to open up China
to European commerce and civilisation.   The politics
of that curious chapter in history, the Negotiations of
Tientsin, are not, however, my task.   Mr Oliphant has,
so far as his official position would admit of, done justice to it in his valuable work.   I have merely to say
that during the month I was living on the Peiho
River there was no perceptible diminution of its volume,
and that the pressure of the monsoon occasioned more
water at high tide on the bar at its entrance in the
month of July than in the month of May.   Towards
the close of June, the plains and Gulf of Pecheli were
swept by violent tornados of short duration; and the
force of wind told me pretty plainly that, in the winter
season, the gales and snow-drifts on these exposed
steppes of northern China must be excessively severe.
What the cold must be of a Pekinese winter, we could
well guess by the profusion of ice everywhere seen in
Tientsin during the whole time of our stay there, and
that, too, in great solid blocks of eight or nine inches
in thickness; but, on the other hand, one could not
help thinking that if that winter was as severe as
winters are said to be in Russia, the whole of the

starving, naked creatures we saw trooping about Tientsin must have been swept off with cold alone. Why
they are not must be added to the host of unexplained
phenomena in this land of oddities.

The only general remarks upon Chili that I have to
add, are touching the climate. Nothing could have
been more invigorating and delicious than the weather
we experienced throughout April and May. Europeans
could work in the sun with perfect impunity, and the
nights were cold enough to wear blue clothing and to
sleep under a blanket. During June, the power of the
sun increased very much, but the nights, particularly
on shore, were still very refreshing. Two hot days
were, in June, invariably followed by a tornado, generally coming from the north-west, which cooled the
atmosphere amazingly.

Dry, hot winds from the desert of Kobi were occasionally experienced; they were not more trying than the
siroccos of the Mediterranean; and, provided no violent
exertion was called for during their continuance, which
never exceeded more than twelve hours, no evil ensued.

The following are the maximum and minimum tem-
peratures registered during eighty-four days off the
Peiho River and in Tientsin:—

			Maximum. ° Fahr.	Minimum. ° Fahr.
Thermometer on board ship,	April		68	46
,,	,,	May	74	50
,,	on shore,	June	86	62
,,	in the ship,	July	98	73

During the same period of eighty-four days—that is,
from the 14th April to the 14th July—the wind prevailed as follows:—

>12 days the wind prevailed from North to East.
>12 days   ,,   ,,   North to West.
>38 days   ,,   ,,   South to East.
>22 days   ,,   ,,   South to West.

Just prior to quitting Tientsin, the temperature rose
to 96° during the day in the shade, and we thought it
very hot; but when in a week subsequently we found
ourselves gasping in the hot, steam-like atmosphere of
the Yang-tze-kiang, all looked back with regret to the
clear and bracing climate we had left behind us in
Northern China.

TIDAL OBSERVATIONS made on board H.M.S. Furious at the anchorage off the Peiho River, Gulf of Pecheli, Lat. 38° 55′ 18″ N., Long. 117° 54′ 30″ E., for the purpose of ascertaining the Rise and Fall on the Bar of that River, and High Water at Full and Change of the Moon.

Date		Moon's Age from Nautical Almanac	High Water Time (h. m.)	High Water Height (ft. in.)	Low Water Time (h. m.)	Low Water Height (ft. in.)	Rise and Fall (ft. in.)	Winds Direction	Winds Force	Weather	Barometer and Thermometer (Deg.)
1858.											
April 15	A.M.	1.5	3 30	31 0	10 15	22 0	9 0	South to S.E.	4 to 5	b c	30.34 / 56
	P.M.		3 45	30 0	11 0	22 6	7 6	S.S.W. to S.S.E.	4 to 5	b q	30.12 / 58
April 16	A.M.	2.5	4 0	31 0	10 30	22 0	9 6	S.S.E. to W.S.W.	2 to 3	o c f	30.11 / 60
	P.M.		4 15	32 0	11 30	23 6	8 6	Calm, W. by S.	0 to 3	c m	30.06 / 60
April 17	A.M.	3.5	4 45	32 0	11 15	22 0	10 0	W.N.W., N.W.	1 to 6	b c	30.09 / 58
	P.M.		5 15	31 0			6 6	N. by W., E. by S.	2 to 6	b c q	29.95 / 62
April 18	A.M.	4.5	4 45	31 0	0 15	24 6	6 0	S.W., W. by N.	2 to 6	h c q	29.97 / 58
	P.M.		6 15	32 0	0 15	22 0	7 0	N.W., Northerly.	6 to 3	b c	29.97 / 62
April 19	A.M.	5.5	5 15	32 0	0 30	25 0	10 0	N. W., N.E.	4 to 1	b c	Not observed
	P.M.		8 0	31 0	1 0	22 0	7 0	South, S.E.	2 to 6	b c q	29.87 / 60
April 20	A.M.	6.5) at 10 P.M. S.T.	4 30	32 0	0 30	24 0	9 3	South-easterly.	5 to 1	b c	29.74 / 60
	P.M.		8 45	31 0	1 45	22 9	9 0	Easterly.	3 to 4	b c	29.82 / 60
April 21	A.M.	7.5	4 45	32 0	1 0	29 0	8 0	E.N.E., East.	5 to 3	b c	29.90 / 58
	P.M.		9 15	31 0	3 0	23 0	7 0	E.S.E. to E.N.E.	1 to 3	c m	29.87 / 60
April 22	A.M.	8.5	8 45	32 0	4 30	25 0	8 6	North-easterly.	3 to 4	b c	30.16 / 58
	P.M.		10 0	32 6	4 15	23 6	8 0	N.N.E.	4 to 6	b c q	30.22 / 54
April 23	A.M.	9.5	9 30	29 6	3 45	26 0	7 0	N.E., N.N.W.	2 to 3	b c	30.14 / 51
	P.M.		11 45	29 0	5 45	22 0	6 0	W.S.W., S.S.W.	2	b c	30.00 / 57
April 24	A.M.	10.5	0 15	29 0	6 15	23 0	7 0	N.W., E.N.E.	3 to 1	b c	30.10 / 60
	P.M.		0 45	31 0	7 30	22 0	6 0	S.E., S.S.E.	3 to 4	b c	29.81 / 61
April 25	A.M.	11.5	1 45	32 0	7 30	24 6	8 6	S.S.E.	2	c r	29.93 / 58
	P.M.		1 45	32 4	7 30	23 0	8 4	West, North.	1 to 4	b c q	30.00 / 59
April 26	A.M.	12.5	2 0	31 0	9 30	24 0	6 0	Easterly, N.W.	2 to 5	b c q	29.95 / 57
	P.M.		2 0	31 6	9 0	22 0	7 0	N.N.W., N.W.	3 to 5	b c	30.03 / 59
April 27	A.M.	13.5	2 0	31 0	9 15	22 0	9 6	N.W.	3 to 5	b c	29.95 / 57
	P.M.		2 15	30 0	9 0	23 6	6 6	N.W.	4 to 6	b c m q	29.97 / 59

TIDAL OBSERVATIONS made on board H.M.S. Furious—*Continued.*

Date		Moon's Age from Nautical Almanac.	High Water Time	High Water Height	Low Water Time	Low Water Height	Rise and Fall	Winds Direction	Force	Weather	Barometer	Thermometer
			h. m.	ft. in.	h. m.	ft. in.	ft. in.				Deg.	
1858. April 28	A.M.	○ at 11 A.M. S.T. 14.5	1 45	30 0	9 45	22 6	7 6	N.W.	3 to 5	b c	30.07	56
	P.M.		3 15	30 6	..	..	.. 6	N.W.	4 to 7	b c q	30.00	60
June 24	A.M.	12.9	..	..	8 30	22 6	6 0	Southerly	1	b c	29.68	76
	P.M.		3 0	31 0	10 0	25 0	7 0	S.E., S.W.	2	b c	29.60	74
June 25	A.M.	13.9	2 30	31 0	8 0	23 0	8 0	S.W.	2 to 4	c p t	29.62	74
	P.M.		4 15	31 0	10 0	28 0	5 0	S.E., N.E.	0 to 2	b c	29.70	75
June 26	A.M.	14.9 ○ at 5 P.M.	2 30	31 0	9 30	23 0	8 0	East, N.W.	1	b c	29.82	74
	P.M.		3 0	31 0	10 0	26 0	5 0	East, S.S.E.	2	b c	29.80	76
June 27	A.M.	15.9	5 0	30 6	10 30	23 0	7 0	E.S.E.	3	c q r	29.75	75
	P.M.		5 0	31 6	10 30	25 0	6 0	South-easterly.		c q r	29.80	75
June 28	A.M.	16.9	5 30	31 0	10 31	23 0	7 0	Northerly.	2 to 3	o c p d	29.71	74
	P.M.		5 30	31 0	11 31	25 0	6 0	N.E.	3 to 1	o c r	29.60	72
June 29	A.M.	17.9	3 30	31 0	11 30	24 0	7 0	N.E.	3		29.55	73
	P.M.		5 30	32 0	12 0	26 6	5 6	E.S.E.	1		29.43	74
June 30		18.9	4 0	30 6	..	..	..	W.S.W., N.W.	2	b c	29.45	75

REMARKS.—The High Water at Full and Change was at 4h. 8m. by our observations; the Russians made it a few minutes later. Difference between day and night tide 18 inches. The highest tide was on the second night tide after Full and Change, sometimes on the third night, according to the winds. Nine feet was the mean of the rise and fall at spring tides with a S.E. breeze; another foot of water was sometimes obtained. During dead neap tides the tides were mainly affected by the winds, and on one occasion a fresh east wind caused as much water on the bar at dead neap as on a spring tide! See Register, April 20, 1858. The flood tide comes from the S.S.E. The ebb tide comes from the N.N.W.

N.B.—We made the High Water at Full and Change at 4h 8m, and no difference between time of High Water at ship or bar. Horsburgh states High Water at Full and Change to be at 3h. 30m. The Admiralty Chart, No. 1891, of A.D. 1840, says 2h. 45m.

SHERARD OSBORN, *Captain* R.N.

CHAPTER II.

APART from all geographical and other information contained in the foregoing notes, there were, in the proceedings that carried myself and others to that previously little known part of China, additional proofs of the truth that the European has ever to use force rather than argument to obtain his ends in China, be they however moderate, however just. Whether we were right or wrong in the Lorcha question, was quite foreign to the object our ambassador had in view in requesting that imperial commissioners might be sent to meet, and treat with him at Shanghai. He merely wanted to put our future relations with the court of Pekin upon such terms as would prevent the recurrence of wars as troublesome as they were scandalous. His proposals were treated with disdain.

We next appear off the entrance of the Peiho River, and again make the simple request that duly authorised envoys might be sent from Pekin. No—first one subterfuge and then another; whilst men, guns, and earthworks increased daily, so as to enable them at their convenience to say begone.

The fortifications of Taku had then to be taken by force of arms, and an armed advance made upon Tientsin.

Commissioners are immediately sent to treat with the allied ambassadors.

The commanders-in-chief, under the impression that the Chinese had thoroughly come to their senses, sent back to their ships the majority of the forces at Tientsin. A reaction immediately set in; an artful attempt was made to induce us to think that the populace were adverse to the concessions demanded by our ambassador. Force had again to be used—men had again to be brought up from the fleet—the ambassadors had to employ threats—the instigator of the reaction had to fly from Tientsin, and was put to death by the Emperor for failing in his vile plot; and again negotiations advanced, simply checked by the obstructive action of America and Russia.

But when that treaty was ready for signature, the imperial commissioners were only induced to sign it through fear of further warlike operations being immediately proceeded with if they failed to do so; and up to the last day—up to the actual signature of that treaty, and even to the receipt of the imperial rescript from Pekin, affirming that he, the Emperor Hienfung, had both read and approved of the terms made by his commissioners—we were bringing up troops, guns, and mortars from Southern China, by way of backing up our arguments, and carrying conviction to the mind of these Chinese, Manchons, and Tartars.

Amongst those, however, who admit these painful facts, there will be two classes of dissentients. 1*st*, Those who point to the action of Russia and America, and fancy that they obtain without other than rational arguments all that we have to win by force of arms.

To these I reply that both Russia and America have used force, though, very wisely, always single-handed; and that they in 1858 merely stood by and saw us knock reason into John Chinaman, and then, with more acuteness than generosity, cried "halves" when the quarry had to be shared. The vigorous and enterprising manner in which Commodore Armstrong, with two ships, entered into hostilities against the province of Canton in 1856, when its able governor - general was holding in check a very large British force, was a case in point. Brother Jonathan, in 1857-58, took good care not to be seen in the very suspicious company of the allied forces of England and France, but he sent one of his largest and biggest frigates, to breathe words of peace and good-will at Tientsin; and although he clasped his

hands and prayed meekly for forgiveness for his sin-
ning brother John, he took very good care to follow
in the wake of John's gunboats, and to introduce that
charming clause in his treaty called the most-favoured-
nation clause, by which saint and sinner shared alike
in the good things of China.

As to the Russians, General Mouravieff was pressing
heavily with an armed heel on the northern frontier of
China, and in a quarter where the Pekinese court was
naturally most susceptible, whilst the sailor-envoy and
ambassador Putiatin was making his treaty at Tientsin. By force Russian generals were tearing from
China a huge morsel of Manchouria and Tartary;
whilst a Russian diplomatist appeared as a man of
peace beside the threatening but still forbearing Englishman in the Peiho River.

We, at anyrate, were frank and above-board; they
were simply humbugs, taking advantage of force without acknowledging that they were indebted to it for all
they acquired from the Chinese.

2d, There is a class, composed of mercantile men,
who accuse us of using force needlessly; who maintain
that we ought to have no political relations with China
—that our sole mission is trade—that our government
should only protect our merchants at the five open
ports.   And lastly, the saints chime in, that the sale

of opium is wicked, and that out of opium has sprung all our wars with China.

To these the reply is simple. Our government tried to have commercial relations alone with China, and utterly failed. British merchants would smuggle—would defraud the Chinese revenue. The Chinese would apply their laws to Englishmen; they seized British subjects as hostages, they threatened our official representative, they fired on our flag, and finally forbid us to trade with them under penalty of death. This was what pure commercial relations brought us to in 1839-40. This, the fruit borne of the East India Company's commercial monopoly, and rapidly ripened under the mercantile energy developed by free-trade.

All subsequent wars have sprung to a very great extent from the same causes,—mercantile rapacity and Chinese official violence, and Chinese incapacity to think or act as Europeans would under similar circumstances. Then, as to the opium-saint—what would he? What will he give the Government of India as a substitute for the ten millions revenue from our opium-farms? And suppose we could say, Perish India! principles before empire—how will he prevent our American brethren importing opium from countries where its production will be immediately developed? Furthermore, what had opium to do with the war be-

tween England and China in 1857-58, and what has it
to do with the present one?

Is our anti-opium friend prepared to not only
comply with the wishes of the Chinese Government
upon the trade in that drug, but in all the rest of our
commerce likewise? because I cannot see where such
morality is to stop. If he is, let him say so, and we
shall be better able to appreciate the patriotism which
would sacrifice a British and intercolonial traffic with
China, amounting to fully one hundred millions sterling! I, for one, say we cannot, we dare not, act in so
suicidal a manner; and that a far wiser course is that
which the allied and neutral powers succeeded at last
in forcing upon the Chinese authorities—namely, to
legalise the opium trade—to impose a tax upon it, and
as heavy a one as they please; and that the Government of China be shown how to raise a legitimate
revenue from foreign commerce, so as to render our
trade as popular with the Emperor and Court, as it is
with the natives of the five open ports.

Whilst, however, I urge that force has to be used in
China to maintain our trade with that empire, whilst
force has to be used to compel the Chinese to act as we
think right, and whilst civilisation alone advances in
that land by dint of force, I am the most earnest advocate for our power not being abused, and that force be
never unjustly or cruelly applied.

That there has been at times an unjust and violent abuse of our power no one can gainsay. We need not enter into a recapitulation of these acts, but simply point out how they may be best avoided for the future.

In the first place, we need a minister resident in Pekin, in direct communication with the court. No expense should be spared to secure the services of a most able person for this office. By that means we get rid of all the petty squabbling between local authorities, out of which, together with mercantile frauds, most of our difficulties have arisen. The Emperor would then be sure to receive a correct version of any local difference—mutual explanations would be possible—at present they are out of the question—and the Emperor, rather than ourselves, might use the stick to enforce civility amongst mandarins, and suppress piracy amongst his own subjects, instead of our soldiers and sailors becoming Chinese policemen, whilst British tax-payers pay the cost.

The next great point should be to convince the British trader that if he defrauds the Chinese Government of the dues and taxes lawfully claimed under treaty, that he shall not be protected by British force; and that some stringent law be enacted for allowing the Chinese to expel from their open ports such British residents as may be proved to have signed false manifests, or otherwise defrauded their

revenue.   At the same time, we ought not to allow
Hong-Kong to be turned into a mere smuggling depot,
whence Chinese products and European manufactures
may be exported or imported to the injury of the
Chinese customs.   Let this be done firmly and
honestly, and let the Chinese officials feel at all places
of trade that we are just traders, be Americans and
Portuguese what they may, and within a few years
the present hostility to us will die out, and maybe
a healthier condition of relations arise between the
Englishman and the Chinaman generally.   These are
the great points which, in the present juncture, I
would urge most earnestly on the British public.   The
first point was provided for in 1858, at Tientsin, by
the British ambassador; there should be no modification of it.   The terrible treachery of Taku in 1859
only too painfully shows how essential it is that we
should know the springs and intentions of the court
of Pekin before its subordinates put to death some
hundreds of our countrymen and involve us in a war ;
whilst, on the other hand, some shameful occurrences
and the shooting down of Chinese customhouse officers
by our traders within the last few months, must convince any one how necessary it is to explain instantly
that England's power shall not be exerted on behalf of
the murderer or smuggler.

   A series of interesting papers, pamphlets, and official

documents connected with China, which have come to
hand from various quarters, place in a pretty clear
light the strange circumstances, the more than Asiatic
treachery, by which the misguided court of Pekin
hoped to escape from the fresh obligations we had
compelled it to undertake in 1858. Those fresh obligations, it must be remembered, were, in the first
place, A British resident in the capital ; (2d), Trade
up the Yang-tze ; and (3d), the right to travel
about China. The objections raised by the Chinese
commissioners to those obligations at the time, and
which objections had to be overruled, were as follows :—

*That Pekin was too hot and dusty for foreigners to
live in ; that the native trade on the Yang-tze would
be ruined ; and, lastly, that the empire was so great
that it would be difficult to apprise the people of the
right of our countrymen to travel !* I need not point
out how thoroughly puerile all these objections were,
or how much they have been subsequently improved
upon by suggestions from other, and I much fear,
European quarters.

With perfect faith in the Emperor's autograph
decree assenting to all the clauses in the treaty of
Tientsin, our allied ambassadors left the Peiho River
in July 1858, with the understanding that in June of
the following year, 1859, ratifications of the treaty

were to be formally exchanged at Pekin, and that its provisions should then come into force.

The *Peking Gazette* contained, in an Imperial decree dated exactly thirty days after the signature of the treaty of Tientsin, the following Chinese version of that treaty, and of our proceedings there :—

"Kweiliang and Hwashana (the imperial commissioners) request us, of our own favour, to reward and encourage those officers, gentry, and merchants who exerted themselves at Tientsin. The barbarians on that occasion had come headlong with their ships up to Tientsin ; but, *moved by the commands of Kweiliang and Hwashana, signified to them with affectionate earnestness, they* (the barbarians) *have now weighed anchor and stood out to sea,*" &c. &c.

No one could hardly be prepared for a government so weak being so rashly false, and they explained away this edict, by supposing that the court of Pekin wished to conceal from the people the humiliation they had been subjected to. At Shanghai the native officials explained it away in that sense. But the fact was, that immediately the presence of our forces was removed from Tientsin, the Emperor and council commenced to think again as Chinamen and Tartars, and decided upon making one more effort to thrust the outer barbarian back into the position he had hitherto held. Of course every Chinese official subordinate sympathised in this desire. Correct information reaching the Emperor would put an end to the system of peculation, extortion, and petty tyranny by which they existed, and by which they each in turn hoped to amass a fortune ; and, sad to say, heeding only their peculiar interests, a large mass of the European mercantile community in China were averse to such relations with the court of Pekin as would compel us to place our trade relations upon a really healthy footing. With few honourable exceptions, they opposed the resident minister in Pekin, extension of open ports, and assistance to the Chinese government in checking fraud upon their customs. In the words of a parliamentary representative of this faction, after having involved us in three wars with China, and endless acts of violence against Chinese officials—" It was not necessary we should go to Pekin for the protection of trade or those engaged in it. If we consulted those concerned in trade in China, we should learn that it is not at Pekin that trade needs protection, but in those ports where commerce is carried on, and where alone British interests should be protected."

Once aware of this sympathy, it was very natural that the Court of Pekin should attempt to reopen negociations at Shanghai upon a treaty which had been formally signed and sealed. If they could only start a discussion upon one clause, they were astute enough to know that that discussion was the introduction of the thin end of the wedge. Unfortunately, our good nature got the better of our right, and a concession was made to some extent. Our representative at Pekin was only to visit it *occasionally*, not to be permanent. We were generous and forbearing, not because we were in the wrong, but purely to gratify the whim, prejudices, or opinions of Chinamen, and we utterly failed in gaining anything by such a course. European diplomacy stood no chance against the cunning, the duplicity, and villany of a Chinese statesman directly that the sword was sheathed.

Every now and then, as subsequent revelations show us, our ambassadors must have been shocked to find that whilst, on the one hand, Kweiliang and Hwashana were all smiles and friendship, the Emperor was urging his officials and subjects in Quangtung to exterminate our garrison in Canton, instead of buying it out, as had been agreed, by paying an indemnity for the destruction of British property in 1856-57. Explanations were at once given—lie on lie was readily proffered to screen the rascality of the court. Accident placed in our hands, about this time, a startling document, which, as subsequent events have proved, only revealed too truly the treachery at work. In some foray of the British garrison out of Canton, our

consul there, Mr Parkes, a most able and energetic
officer, obtained a paper, which appeared to be written
by a native spy, placed in Shanghai to give information of the true state of relations with the English,
to Hwang, governor-general of the Quang provinces.
This emissary, who evidently had struck at the real
intentions of the court of Pekin, reported as follows :
"That relations with the barbarian was entirely in
the hands of three great princes at Pekin ; that the
Emperor was furious at the treaty which had been
forced upon him ; and that the commissioners Kweiliang and Hwashana were sent down to Shanghai to
cancel it at any cost ! but that Ho (an officer of high
rank) had dissuaded the Emperor from doing so for
the present, as it would instantly involve them in a
war." The consequence was the adoption of a milder
course, in which the commissioners were ordered to reopen a discussion upon the three clauses to which I
have already referred. The report went on to say,
that the commissioners had succeeded "in making the
visit of the European representative an occasional one,
in hampering the circulation of travellers in the interior with a system of passports, for which application must be made to native authorities, but that they
had failed in doing anything upon the question of the
opening of the Yang-tze !" Having reported progress
to the Emperor, he expressed himself far from satisfied

with their success, and desired them to try again for
farther concessions.

As the report of a mere spy, it was then difficult to
ascertain how much truth or falsehood there was in
such document; but, standing where we do in 1860,
it serves at once to explain the gross villany of the
Emperor, and makes us regret that any discussion of
the treaty of Tientsin was ever submitted to at Shanghai. Had we simply told the commissioners that,
coute qui coute, we would hold them to their bargain
of 1858—that no demands had then been made but
what had been long and carefully weighed—and that
we were convinced that they were as much for the
good of China as of Britain—there is now but little
doubt on my mind that the imperial commissioners
would either have advised the Emperor to swallow the
treaty, distasteful as it might be, or have had to throw
off the mask, and officially repudiate the treaty of
Tientsin.

The scheme of the Imperial Commissioners to
vitiate rather than utterly break away from the treaty
of Tientsin, was frustrated by Lord Elgin being obliged
suddenly to proceed to Canton; but the Emperor still
skilfully disguised his real intentions, by actually re-
moving a hostile mandarin from office on the repre-
sentations of our Ambassador. This act completed
the duplicity of the court; and we fancied that all

that now remained to be done was to exercise
a little firmness, and the treaty would pass into
law. The Imperial Commissioners had thus fairly
misled Lord Elgin as to the Emperor's intentions
and good faith, while the Emperor, at his own convenience, prepared to repudiate his engagements.
June 1859 found our new envoy, Mr Bruce, with a
respectable naval cortège under Admiral Hope, off
the entrance of the Peiho River. There was no one
to receive them ; the river was barred with stupendous
booms and barriers ; they attempted to pass through,
and fell into an ambuscade. Our squadron was repulsed with a loss of 500 killed and wounded, and
the treaty of Tientsin had virtually to be worked out
again. If this is not a tale of deep duplicity, crowned
by an act of cruel treachery, I should like to know
how to define it.

Shanghai is only forty-two days by the overland
route from Charing Cross ; and at the entrance of the
Peiho River I met a traveller, in 1858, who was only
fifty days from Paris ; yet, strange to relate, although
by the middle of last September we knew of a foul
dishonour to our flag ; although we then learned that
the blood of four hundred slain, the prestige of the
navy, and the honour of the insulted representative of

our Sovereign, called for retribution, nothing has as yet been done to wipe off this sorrow and shame, and punish such treachery. Napoleon the Third was the first to speak ; Paris, not London. On March 1, 1859, nine months after the occurrence, that monarch informed the world that " a serious expedition, combined with the forces of Great Britain, would chastise China for her perfidy." Our last news from China, up to May 1859, do not lead us to believe that this chastisement will be inflicted before the hot weather sets in, when it must be necessarily delayed until August, and in the mean time we have tamely asked China for an apology, an ultimatum which she has treated with deserved contempt; and before a blow has been struck, an allied expedition, fitted out for an apology, has already cost nearly four millions sterling ! Never in the annals of English history was there such procrastination combined with such a fearful expenditure. Every one asks what can have occasioned it.

Great Britain, ever ready to cover the seas with her fleets, did not surely require all this time to avenge a defeated squadron ? We may hope that, had our admiral been repulsed or defeated by a Russian force, instead of Chinese forts, on the 24th June 1859, we should not have had to look in vain, as we did in the last Indian mails, for the intelligence of the punishment of the foe. It is evidently a feigned appearance of want of energy and readiness; and woe betide France or Russia if they estimate our preparation by the late display. Unreasonable people might say that, with the steam-navies of England afloat in the East, and in the Mediterranean, as well as idle in our home ports, together with the use of electric telegraphs, a better display of energy and combination might have been effected;—one which would have shown Europe, where every nation is closely watching us, and marking how we are likely to come out of the great fight hereafter to be fought for the supremacy of the seas and the commerce of the world — that England's naval and military forces can be concentrated with greater rapidity than ever, and protect with overpowering force any point at which her interests or her honour may be threatened. In a military or strategical point of view, delay has only multiplied our difficulties. With a Chinaman, as with any other Eastern, delay in acting against him, when he assumes a hostile position, does not increase the chance of his taking a more enlightened view of the irrational nature of his own proceedings, but merely confirms him in his own folly, and he considers your forbearance to arise from fear or hesitation. The victory of Taku, accomplished by the war-party of Pekin, instead of bringing down immediately upon its perpetrators the vengeance of Great Britain, was mildly followed by a request for an explanation and an apology. The breach of the treaty of Teintsin, which our representatives had in 1858 tried to persuade Hwashana and Kweiliang would infallibly involve the Emperor in a war with the Allies, was found only to bring a long despatch from our representative in China, and, coupled with it, the comments of certain writers in England, who seemed to see no dishonour to their country in the defeat of its navy. All this must have naturally served to cheer on the faction in Pekin who represent the obstructionists of China; and every hour of delay has only served to still farther confirm their strength, and enabled them to meet our threats of vengeance. I believe that every province of China has contributed its quota of men, money, or material, towards multiplying the difficulties we shall find in making the Emperor Hienfung fulfill his engagements. He has had a whole twelvemonth to concentrate these means ; and I know that the customs-dues paid by the foreign trade alone of Shanghai during that same period has been nearly one and a quarter millions sterling—or, in other words, that European merchants have been contributing that sum to the Chinese exchequer, to be employed in resisting the demands of Her Majesty's Government, and destroying our soldiers and sailors.

I may speak feelingly as a naval officer; but I say if

this is Christian forbearance and humanity, I should
like those who have most faith in such principles to
lead the next forlorn hope over the mud flats of Taku
into the jaws of Prince Sing-o-losin's batteries.

I take it for granted that our Secretary of State for
Foreign Affairs approved the treaty of Tientsin. He
has said as much—nay, lately expressed a desire to see
it ratified. He knew that his subordinate, Mr Bruce,
in attempting to obtain that ratification, had been
violently and insolently received, and that the Chinese
government did then, and have since, repudiated
every one of the concessions in the treaty which
rendered it of the slightest value to us. He has subsequently approved of the proceedings of Mr Bruce,
and, in common with his Queen, and the heads and
representatives of this great country, lauded the noble
self-sacrifice and heroic devotion of the small band of
seamen who essayed, in June 1859, to punish the
perfidious Court of Pekin. Yet up to this hour, we
have dawdled and hesitated, in the hope that the
Emperor of China would give us a loophole—however mean, mattered little—out of which to escape
from the difficulty of reasserting our own dignity ; and
that assertion of our dignity, after the Emperor Napoleon had shown what the French policy was to be,
amounted to this,—that if the Emperor of China
would apologise for the slaughter of four hundred

Englishmen, the destruction of our vessels, and the defeat of our squadron, we would be content with a simple ratification — no indemnity for the past, no guarantees for the future. Was this, I ask, worthy of Great Britain? or worth the four millions spent in trying to obtain it? Mark what is the issue of such a policy. Our expenses have been enormous, our troops are suffering from long confinement on ship-board, and two vessels full of invalids are already reported as arrived at the Cape, in the very same mail from the East which records the fact that the Court of Pekin has treated the proposals of our diplo-matists with scorn! Have we not richly merited this last act of contempt?

Let me strive to throw some light upon the causes which have occasioned delay in the first place, and then the adoption of a milk-and-water policy, which at the end of a twelvemonth leaves us in a worse position than when the affair commenced. I have told how between the signing of the treaty of Tientsin and the signing of the new tariff at Shanghai, a steady in-trigue against the three great clauses—direct official intercourse at Pekin, extension of trade to other ports, and the right to travel through China—was fomented by certain native and European monopolists, who hav-ing a great interest in the present condition of Chinese traffic, were loth to see changes which might lessen,

and assuredly could not increase, their huge profits.
The joy and excitement in great Britain at the news
of the opening of the vast empire of China was too
earnest, too genuine, to allow those selfish counsels to
have much influence at home, until the destruction of
that treaty was brought about in China. But out in
China they in no way disguised their open hostility to
the nobleman who had negotiated that treaty : they
tried to discover and publish every flaw in it ; and
they were quite as obstructive to Lord Elgin in 1857,
'58, '59, as the blue-books show the same faction to
have been to Sir Henry Pottinger in 1843, '44. Lord
Elgin was looked upon as an enemy to certain vested
rights, and those vested rights went into opposition,
and stood arrayed against the interests of Great Britain
and against the treaty of Tientsin. They consequently
aided and abetted (whether directly or indirectly matters little) the Emperor and mandarins in their deter-
mination to subvert that treaty. Learning, as the
mandarins stationed at the open ports could easily do,
that the majority of the leading mercantile firms were
well satisfied with the terms of the treaty of Nankin,
that they only wanted a modification of the tariff, and
that they were quite as averse as the natives to a
general opening up of China, what so natural, but
that they should have felt that they had a strong
party in their favour, and that their co-operation was

certain in any attempt to blow up the treaty of
Tientsin.

The Emperor, fully enlightened upon this subject,
made a bold stroke to shake himself clear of the engagements entered into.   The public in England,
astounded at the sudden and unexpected perfidy, as
well as the desperate nature of the combat in which
the Emperor broke through his treaty, turned naturally
for an explanation of the tragedy to those who had
been living longest amongst the Chinese.   Then it was
that we saw this Chinese vested interest paralysing
the councils of our sovereign, the strong arm of the
executive, and the sound sense of the English public.
Strange that people having to choose between class
and imperial interests should halt between the two.
Yet so it is.   Even Lord Elgin had to throw a sop to
this rampant interest as he left our shores ; and we
meet it in all quarters, under all shapes and guises.
The English merchants engaged in the Chinese trade
are not perhaps very numerous, but they are extremely
wealthy, and possess, for their numbers, great interest.
Firms that can allow members to retire on from fifty
to a hundred thousand pounds in the course of every
few years, are by no means despicable either in family
connection, social position, or territorial status, in
Great Britain ; and the fight they are now making,

and the specious arguments they advance on behalf
really of their vested interests, have induced our
statesmen to steer a middle course, which has up to
this day signally failed. They beg us to let things
be. Provided we correct a few of the most glaring
defects in the old tariff, they would be well content to
see the streams of commerce flow as they do at present. They want us to accept as inevitable a chronic
state of petty hostility between consuls and mandarins,
a triennal war, periodic captures of Canton, burnings of
British mercantile dwellings, and exaction of large in-
demnifications. They allow that it may be an inconvenience to the Exchequer, an injustice and hardship to
the tax-payer at home, to pay the expenses of these
petty wars. But is not that better, their wisdom tells
them, than an extension of British relations with China,
which shall stop all smuggling?—is not that better
than an immense influx of fresh merchants and fresh
capital, with increased competition, lower prices, and
lower profits? It is true that the imports of England
into China are as nothing compared to the exports, and
the balance of trade against us at Shanghai in 1859
amounted to five and a quarter millions;* but what

---

* The legitimate exports of Shanghai during 1859 were £11,950,080,
against an import of only £6,713,627 sterling; and Shanghai only represents a third of the European trade with China.

care they ? Their profits consist in the *export* of tea and silk ; and the more limited the area from which tea and silk are drawn, the more scarce the article may be made to appear, and the higher the price that can be exacted. Never did monopoly establish herself more firmly under the guise of free-trade, than she has done in the trade of the five ports of China—never were specious arguments more plentiful on behalf of a close corporation, than will be and have been advanced by those directly interested in the present trade of China. It is their objections and their influence which have alarmed the Foreign Secretary of Great Britain, and which at this moment threaten to sacrifice the interests of the manufacturer and consumer at home to the vested rights of the *exporters* from China. I do not believe that they will, in the long-run, succeed in their policy. The sound good-sense of this country will out-ride eventually all their jog-along theories. But what I desire to see is, that whilst we have a good opportunity, and right is on our side, that the policy pursued in China be worthy, in the first place, of the dignity and honour of Great Britain, and that the interests and pockets of the heavily taxed millions at home be consulted, instead of that of a hundred commercial magnates, who retail us tea and silk at cent per cent profits.

I do not mean for a moment to say that the Anglo-

Chinese traders are worse than any other monopolists ;
I merely desire to point out that their instincts are the
preservation of present profits—not the interests of this
empire, of Christianity, or civilisation. Even in a
purely commercial point of view, a higher authority
than myself has declared of these monopolists, that
"their calculations do not extend beyond their business. Why should they ? They send home produce
and receive its value. They do not feel the inconvenience occasioned to Europe by a constant and unvarying
trade-wind which blows semi-monthly cargoes of silver
into the ports of a hoarding nation." *

Let me, therefore, as one who has paid some attention to the subject, state the grounds upon which I
believe the opening of China, as it will be opened when
the treaty of Tientsin comes into full force, is a question of vital importance to England, and to the manufacturers and consumers living within her borders ; and
that the rapid extension of trade which will follow
an energetic and determined policy at Pekin, will
more than repay us for our present expense, and the
pain and the annoyance of a third series of allied
operations.

Let our reader spread before him a map of China,
and, the better to appreciate the size and area of that

* See chap. xvii. of *China in* 1857-58, by Geo. Wingrove Cooke.
Routledge & Co., London.

empire, he must remember that it is about equal to Europe, supposing the latter was a square, without including the Iberian Peninsula.   But bear in mind that China is blessed with a far richer soil, abounding in products which Europe has to send for from every quarter of the globe ; and that if between the Ural Mountains and the Atlantic, between the Frozen Ocean and the Mediterranean, we can muster three hundred millions of inhabitants, China can boast of four hundred millions, living under one form of government, one written language, and one code of laws.   This vast country, this heaving mass of living creatures, is placed at the most remote point of the globe with respect to Europe ; it wants nothing from us, though we require much from it.   There is not a province in China which does not produce some article of actual necessity or luxury for Europe, and at the same time, out of the eighteen provinces which China is divided into, there are as yet only four,* situated on the south-east seaboard, to which Europeans have obtained access, and even their resources are but very partially known. Access to these four provinces only dates back to 1842 : and prior to that, from the year 1549 (for three centuries, in short), all the trade of Europe with the great Empire of China was restricted to a single port in the province of Canton.   We have but to turn back to the

* Quang-tung, Fokien, Chekiang, and Kiang-su.

parliamentary debates, the pamphlets and writings of 1830-1840, to be able to point out, almost word for word, the very same arguments against the extension of trade beyond Canton, and of the danger of touching a commerce so lucrative to the merchant and beneficial to the Exchequer, as are at present being used to frighten us from any further progress in a direction which experience tells us is the right one.

Since we have traded with four, instead of one province in China, the tea-trade of Britain has more than tripled, and nearly all that tea comes from a limited area, which may be best defined by drawing a line *northward* from Canton, and *westward* from Shanghai, until they meet. The portion of China enclosed by those two lines represents the region from which we procure nearly all our teas. But do not suppose that the Chinese of all the rest of China are dependent upon this same district for tea : no, nearly all China produces quite as good tea, but the price of carriage, and the distance from the five open ports, place the purchase of those teas out of our power. In proof of this, we will quote the Russian tea-trade, which may now be called the Siberian trade, Russia proper having wisely decided upon abandoning the overland route for her commerce, and is now about to enter as a competitor in the same markets as ourselves. This Siberian tea-

trade has increased 57½ per cent within the last ten
years. The teas are exported from the remote north-
west provinces of Stzchuen, Kansoo, and Shansi; they
are of the best quality, for the good descriptions will
only pay for the expensive land-carriage ; and we know
that in 1850 nearly ten million pounds of tea were carried out of China by this route, and that the supply was
simply limited to the demand ;—had fifty times as much
been required, it would have been forthcoming. In the
bygone year, we find that Great Britain exported from
China nearly fifty-five million pounds of teâ, an increase over the year '58 of nigh upon thirty million
pounds ; and that the United States, in like manner,
carried off twenty-three and a quarter million pounds
of tea, or five million pounds increase. Yet for all
this the myriads of China have nowhere missed their
constant beverage, whilst the poor artisan's home in
Europe still often lacks it, in consequence of its great
price. The consumption of tea is everywhere increasing ; its imports into Europe and America are steadily
multiplying ; the price of the article in England, apart
from the dues levied upon it by our customs, is still
excessive. The very tea that the wife of the poor
English labourer pays 2s. 10d. or 3s. a-pound for—
and even at that price it is adulterated with every
abomination under heaven—sells on the spot where it
is produced at 80 cash per catty, or in rough terms,

3d. a-pound English.* Who is it that takes the remaining 2s. 6d. for delivering a pound of tea at our doors? Is it the mandarin, the merchant, or Mr Gladstone? One thing is very certain, that the half-crown does not go into the hands of the poor Chinese tea-farmer, and that it comes out of the hard-earned wages of the English labourer, or starving half-pay officer. The *Times*, through its correspondent, let us, two years since, into some of the secrets of the tea trade; we commend his information, since republished in the form of a book, to the attention of all tea consumers. We are there shown, in the twenty-third chapter, how wonderfully skilful the Chinese authorities have become in abstracting revenue from teas, directly they found them passing from hand to hand as an article of foreign commerce. We are told that in the beginning—nay, until very lately—the only tax upon tea was in the form of a small impost, levied as a land-tax at so much per rood, paid by the tea-grower; and that if it passed to Shanghai through the provincial capital Hang-chow-foo, a registry tax of 3 cents per 133 lb. was exacted for the benefit of the local government; but that at this hour that tax has been increased to 3d. per pound!—thus at once

---

* Taking 1200 cash as equal to 4s. 2d., or a dollar, and the catty at a pound and a quarter English. Our authority as to the price of tea is Mr Fortune's valuable work, *The Tea Districts of China.*

doubling the original cost of the tea ; besides which, every district between the point of growth and port of export takes an additional *" squeeze "* out of us, until nearly 6d. per pound is paid in dues upon tea originally worth only 3d. per pound.

Now it is evident from this, that to have cheap tea we must buy our teas upon the tea-farms, and pay one fair tax instead of a dozen irregular ones. As a proof of how we gain by proximity to the tea-bearing districts, we are informed that every chest of tea embarked at Foo-chow-foo escapes with exactly thirteen shillings per chest less transit-tax than those passing to Shanghai ; and Mr Wingrove Cooke very justly estimates that, if we could (as we shall do by the Treaty of Tientsin) ascend the Yang-tze-Kiang, and at Hankow, or on the shores of the Poyang and Tunting lakes, embark our own purchases of the Houpak teas, we should save exactly 60s. of transit-duty upon every 133 lb. of the leaf. The Treaty of Tientsin, in Articles 9, 10, and 28, exactly meets our wants in this respect. We are thereby granted " the right to travel for pleasure or purposes of trade to all parts of the interior of China," and " no opposition shall be offered to the traveller or merchant in the hiring of persons or vessels for the carriage of their baggage or merchandise." " British merchant-ships shall have authority to trade upon the Yang-tze ; " and " it shall be at

the option of any British subject, desiring to convey
produce purchased inland to a port, or to convey
imports from a port to an inland market, to clear his
goods of all transit-duties by payment of a *single*
charge," and "the amount of this charge shall be cal-
culated as nearly as possible at the rate of 2½ per
cent *ad valorem!*" There is only one flaw in these
important Articles, namely, that the clause (10) with
respect to the opening of the Yang-tze for our shipping is made contingent upon the suppression of
rebellion in China! This defect Lord Elgin should
be directed to remedy; all such clauses of any future
Treaty should come at once into action; and we can,
as neutrals, pass and repass the rebel posts without let
or hindrance to the military proceedings of Taepings
or Imperialists.

Does any sane person suppose that we, the consumers at home, have not a large and direct interest
in this promised condition of the tea trade? By
it alone we may hope to pay less for a beverage
which has become almost a necessary of life in every
English household, and a most important article of
national consumption—and be it remembered that the
consumption represents annually, in money, the gross
amount of six millions sterling, even if there was not
a pound of tea consumed in England at more than 3s.
a-pound. On the other hand, it is equally certain

that the wholesale importers of tea into this country must have every reason to be perfectly satisfied with their present profit, and, if appealed to for information, that they should very naturally say,—"Pray, let us alone; have a little war when it suits us, for the purpose of striking a balance, working off old stocks, or screening certain deficiencies." Periodic panics are beneficial in a rise of the price of opium, and a fall in that of tea and silk amongst the Chinese, who fear that the markets will be closed; whilst in London prices rise on those same articles because they expect a deficiency.

Thus it is that we seek in vain from those who are China traders for information relative to the price of tea on the places of growth; thus it is that we see no suggestions emanating from them as to the means whereby its cost may be diminished to the English consumer; thus it is that they do not give cordial support to the servants of this empire, when they are striving to open up a vast region, from whence a four-fold quantity of tea or silk may be procured, and where the natives may be induced to take English manufactures instead of English silver in exchange; and thus it is that we find them unwilling to pay the lawful fiscal dues to the Chinese government, and objecting to all "raprochement" between the two governments as likely to sign the death-warrant of the

present huge smuggling system, and petty wars as
unworthy of Britain as they ought to be distasteful to
every right-minded soldier and sailor.

But to return to the Chinese exports, the reader must
remember that, in dealing with the tea question, and
pointing out the advantages likely to accrue to the
public from the opening up of China upon that article
alone, we have merely selected it as an example from
many other Chinese *exports* to which the argument
is equally applicable. Silk, for instance, is plentiful
over two-thirds of the area of China — the upper
classes wear it quite as much in the great province
of Stz-chuen, and as generally, as they do in Quang-
tung. The holiday suit of the shop-boy in Pecheli
is of silk, as well as that of the servants in Amoy or
Shanghai.

All the reasonable hopes and expectations of diminished cost to the home consumers in the future
supply of these Chinese products, if the Elgin Treaty
be faithfully and fully carried out, apply in a fourfold
ratio to the question of our imports to China.

At the present moment we may be said to pay in
silver for nearly all the products of China, and for
years it has been the gulf into which all the silver
currency of Europe has been pouring. To check this
drain, our great object must be to encourage the import into China of such articles of home and colonial

produce as shall in some degree preserve a healthy balance of trade.

There are two sorts of imports which are in some demand in China, all of *which, when we can deliver upon the spot where they are needed,* will, we believe, be required in vast quantities.

The first is British colonial produce, such as opium, rice, cotton, " Straits produce," and sundry Eastern luxuries. The second is British home manufacture of cotton and wool, iron, lead, and tin, wrought, or in bars and pigs.

With respect to the first class of imports in China, the trade may be said to be steadily increasing, and they alone return nearly ten millions sterling of the great balance against us. Opium, however, figures by far the highest in that return trade. The second class of imports—those from Britain—are at a stand-still, and about one and a half millions sterling represent the annual amount of the manufactures of this country taken by China during the last five or six years.

As yet we have only trustworthy trade-returns for one port in China : that one port is Shanghai, where, thanks to the zeal and rectitude of Mr Lay, who so distinguished himself in bringing about the signature of the Treaty of Tientsin, there is now established an Anglo-Chinese customhouse, which insures the honest payment to the native authorities of all lawful dues.

From the custom returns there published under Mr
Lay's supervision, and Mr Wingrove Cooke's writings,
as well as the Parliamentary Blue-Books, we learn
some startling facts touching the exports and imports
of that one port, and they serve as a clue to that of
Canton, where there has been mystification, smuggling,
and, we much fear, great fraud. In the year 1857,
we find that the entire trade in foreign bottoms carried on in Shanghai was represented as £26,774,018 :
the portion of that trade due to imports was only
£3,010,500 sterling, apart from opium, and *but* for
that much-abused drug, we should have had to pay
nigh upon *fourteen millions sterling* for the vast
amount of tea and silk carried to Europe from that
seaport alone ; and as it was, the opium sold only
reduced that figure to about nine millions sterling.
Perhaps 1857 was an exceptional year, and the failure
of the silk crop in Europe occasioned a greater demand
than may again occur for Chinese silk ; if so, we may
point to the trade returns of '56, where the import of
bullion amounted to four and a quarter millions sterling,
to settle the balance of trade in Shanghai.   During the
past year, 1859, the increase of exports of Chinese
produce from Shanghai alone is very marked, according to the returns I have just received.   In tea alone
it amounts to 9,863,029 lb. ! or just a fourth of the
entire amount consumed by Great Britain and her

colonies when the East India Company had the monopoly; and in silk, the increase in 1859 amounts to
4373 bales—but in our articles of manufacture imported into Shanghai I can find no proportionate
increase. The difference, of course, has to be paid in
hard coin, and but for the ten millions in bullion re-
covered from the Chinese by the sale of opium, the
effect upon our currency would be startling. For years
Europe has been pouring her bullion into the lap of
China, in return for her much-needed products. It is
China that has absorbed and hoarded all the great
silver currency which the mines of Mexico and Peru
disseminated over the world. China has recently absorbed nearly all the French silver currency, as fast as
it has been issued; and we are only indebted to our
Indian products for recovering some fraction in return
payment for our opium, rice, cottons, and sugars.

Now it stands to reason that it is rather the business
of people at home, than of the traders upon the spot, to
find some better substitute for the payment of Chinese
products than the silver currency of Europe. The
merchant in China acts as the mere broker between
the producer and the consumer. If the consumer
chooses to be satisfied with paying in bullion, *tant
mieux* for the broker; the fluctuations in exchange are
a vast source of profit, having ranged in China from
4s. 4d. to 6s. per dollar. The consumer knows nothing

of those mysteries, and has as little to do with the advantages accruing as the poor tea-grower. Bullion is a convenient and rapid form of exchange for produce, it bears "sweating" in so many ways; and the Chinese tea-broker prefers it to goods, because, having brought his teas down from a far country, he can carry back silver easier than anything else; and in that land of "squeezes" he can better conceal his profits from the keen-eyed mandarin, when those profits are in a hard mass of bullion, than if he was returning into the interior escorted by coolies carrying bales of British manufacture. Piracy, rebellion, and robbery are the normal condition of this vast empire, and it is that as much as the venality of the authorities which checks the circulation of our calicoes and woollens, our hardware and crockery.

We are aware that it is the fashion to say, "Oh! the Chinese are a manufacturing nation, and although the power-loom has beat all the rest of the world, it must yield before Chinese manual industry." We believe this to be simple nonsense. The natives of India were manufacturers of calico until we entered the field against them. The squaws of North America were likewise manufacturesses until Yankee drills came into the market. The South Sea islanders made "tappa" far cheaper than we once could afford to clothe them; and the Peruvian, Chilian, and Araucanian

weaved " ponchos," until Manchester put her shoulder
to the work, and beat the handloom out of the most
remote valleys of the Andes.   And when was it that
the European manufacturer thus succeeded ? We reply,
when he was able to compete against native industry
in supplying native wants directly *in* the native market
—not at some remote point a thousand miles from it,
where his article was loaded with heavy expenses inci-
dent to land-carriage, or exorbitant and unjust taxes—
and that is exactly the position in China that we must
strive to attain.   To sell our manufactures, we must
deliver them upon the spot where they are required—
that is, in every province of China ; and as I have
before said, to have cheap Chinese products we must
buy them at the places of growth.

At present our trading stations are situated on the
remote confines of a land as large as Europe, the interior of which, beyond that we know it to be very fertile
and very populous, we are supremely ignorant of.   We
are required to land woollens in the tropics for the use
of a people living in a remote corner of the empire,
where the winters are most severe.   Fancy, for instance, if a trader who desired to compete with the
woollen manufactures of St Petersburg, was compelled
to land them at Bayonne, and pay for the carriage, as
well as to bribe fifty customhouses, before they reached
the Neva : would he think it strange if his cloth could

not in price compete with the native article under such
circumstances? Yet our position, so far as the woollen
trade with China is concerned, is exactly similar. We
know that the inhabitants of the region in which the
five ports are situated do not need our cloths; but we
have to land them at Canton or Shanghai, in the hope
of their reaching Pekin, or the still more remote and
rigorous climates of Kansoo and Shansi! As yet we
have had no seaport, no access to all that portion of
China, inhabited by some two hundred millions of
souls, in which the severity of the winter renders it
likely that they need our woollens.

The arguments which apply to the introduction of
our woollen manufactures into China, apply with still
greater force to the cheap productions of our cotton
manufactories. We need not reiterate them, but will,
from the table of exports and imports found in the
remote city of Hankow, when it was visited by Lord
Elgin,* point out an interesting fact or two, to show
why the cotton manufactures of Great Britain will not
compete with the native ones, until we deliver them
cheaper at the interior marts.

It will there be seen that a piece of common grey
sheeting, 38½ yards long and 39 inches broad, is sold
by our merchants at Shanghai for about 12s., or say,

* See Appendix III., vol. ii. p. 493, *Lord Elgin's Mission to China
and Japan.* By LAURENCE OLIPHANT, Esq.

roughly, 4d. a yard; the same material was selling in
the Hankow shops for 6½d. or $\frac{132}{1000}$ part of 52 pence
per yard; an increase of 2½ per yard, or 6s. 4d. per
piece, that increased price being simply due to a land
or water transit of about six hundred miles into China;
and the material would have treble that distance to
travel before it could reach the farther borders of the
empire. Yet, in spite of its price, this material was
selling, and, we were told, was in much use for many
common purposes. Now the native manufacture of
an equally common description, though only 10½
inches wide, was being retailed in that same city of
Hankow for about 2d. per yard; it would require, of
course, three breadths, a yard long, of that material,
to render it equal to a yard of our sheeting. The
result, therefore, was, that a quantity of English
manufacture at Hankow, which cost 6½d., had to
compete with a native material, coarser, it is true;
but stronger, which cost 6d., and yet it did do so
with considerable success; and we may safely say,
that when our cottons are delivered at Hankow at a
more reasonable rate of profit, the consumption of
them must increase amazingly.

It is truly monstrous to suppose, if our merchants
find it worth while to export a distance of 17,000
miles a piece of manufacture to Shanghai, and retail
it there for 12s., that a Chinese broker is to carry it

only 600 miles into the interior, and extort from his countrymen 18s. 4d. for it. It is this extortion, and not the handloom industry of China, which has so long left unfulfilled the just expectations of Great Britain in relation to her export trade with China. The extraordinary charges upon the common manufacture which we have given as an example, were still more gross, when we take into consideration the Hankow prices of English chintz, brocades, and twills.

Manchester chintz, selling at about 7d. a yard at Shanghai, was selling at 10¾d. per yard in Hankow; brocades, worth 7d. a yard in Shanghai, were being retailed at an additional 5d. per yard profit; or the trader from the western provinces of China who visited Hankow had to pay 40s. for a piece of English manufacture, which we could have sold him at a profit in Shanghai for 24s. These figures ought to satisfy us that the Chinese native monopolists at the seaports have no small interest at stake in confining us to the frontier, where our places of commerce are now situated; and we have pretty good proof of what we have before stated, that the attention and energy of our merchants have as yet been mainly directed to the exporting of Chinese products, and not to the introduction of the fruits of British labour. Access to the interior of China, and access to every province of China, we now have by treaty-right—it is all we need

to fully succeed in being to her what we are to nearly all
the rest of the world—her manufacturer. The millions
within the rich borders of the Central Land will hail our
arrival amongst them. It is alone the official and the
monopolist who are against us. To them pressure must
be applied ; in doing that we need not harm the industrious and sympathising masses. Yet we must not
fail to impress upon all, that though we be traders as
they are, as anxious for gain and as keen in questions
of profit, we are, at the same time, much to be pre-
ferred as friends, and most troublesome and warlike
enemies ; and the Hong merchant and retired mandarin, who pay the starving labourer to don the dress
and arms of a brave, and urge him to resist the inva-
sion of free trade and European civilisation, must be
clearly shown, what they do not yet understand, that
the Englishman who shall boldly throw himself into
the heart of China on behalf of his country's interests
as well as his own, on the faith of the engagements
made with its Government, must be justly treated.
On the other hand, we ought not to fail to do all in
our power to prevent our traders being smugglers,
and insist that they shall pay all lawful dues, and
conform to the laws as far as a Christian may do
so. This, we argue, may be all easily brought about
by a summary punishment of the Court of Pekin
for its late perfidy, by insisting upon our right of

having a representative at Pekin, who shall communicate directly with the prime-minister or sovereign ; and, lastly, by giving all countenance and support to the establishment of the new-raised Chinese and European boards of customs in China—a measure which we are happy to see advancing steadily, in spite of much covert as well as open opposition.

CHAPTER III.

I POINTED out in the last chapter the limited portion of the vast Empire of China to which our trade is at present restricted, and endeavoured to show how it came to pass that the native as well as the foreign monopolist, dwelling on the seaboard of the four accessible provinces of China, were averse or indifferent to a farther prosecution of military operations for the enforcement of a Treaty which laid open to the European every part of the Flowery Land.

I have tried in general terms to point out how much Imperial interests are involved in the extension of our commerce, and right to trade with every part of China, and that every clause in that Treaty of Tientsin ought to be exacted to the fullest extent. We shall yet, I hope and trust, enforce that treaty, and punish those who broke the peace it promised. Let me endeavour to show how much an energetic and prudent series of military and naval operations are necessary for British interests, and may be carried out in Northern China—that is, north of, and beyond, all our present mercantile establishments—with this twofold object:—

First, To open up rich regions, populated by Asiatics in a high state of Eastern civilisation, all of whom will become our customers; and that the impression made on their minds by Englishmen appearing among them in a military character, will tend to the future security and profit of our missionary and merchant.

Secondly, To impress upon an Eastern Court the grand fact, that the defeat of the forces of Great Britain, and the slaying and wounding of four hundred and fifty British subjects, is not an act to be passed over with a tame apology, without indemnity, or without guarantee against its recurrence, when perhaps some unfortunate collection of traders shall fall under the wrath of Emperor or mandarins.

These two objects are so interwoven one with the other, that it is impossible to consider them separately. You cannot open China but as an armed man—victorious. You cannot teach the rulers of China to respect their political engagements with a foreigner, except through fear. It is because I wish to open China, to see our import trade *to* China as flourishing as the export trade *from* China, that I urge an armed exploration of her seaboard and interior; and I can-

not help thinking that those who are now declaiming
against such measures on the plea of humanity, consult
rather their ledgers than their consciences in desiring
to prevent the introduction, now that an opportunity
occurs, of a better civilisation and a purer creed
amongst the many millions who long for our coming,
but who are forbidden to hold intercourse with us by
the edicts of the Brother of the Moon. God forbid
that England should appear armed at the Peiho merely
to wreak vengeance upon stolid mandarins or their
barbarous followers. Nothing could be more horrible
or unnatural than such a spirit of revenge—it is
not that I advocate ; but we know that whilst, on
the one hand, experience has taught us that it is false
humanity to allow an Asiatic despot to suppose he
may insult or slay a Christian with impunity—on the
other hand, "Providence, that doth shape our ends,"
has never caused us to vindicate the claims of Western
civilisation without our leaving behind us abundant
and living proofs of our desire to improve the races
we have come in contact with. I therefore believe—
and it will be nothing new in the history of our
country—that the march of our legions in Shantung and
Pechelee, and the explorations of our sailors in the
Yang-tze river and Yellow Sea, will be but the prelude
to a condition of things over which the merchant and
philanthropist shall rejoice, and future Chancellors of

the Exchequer congratulate themselves on our having
at any rate legislated somewhat for posterity.

Perhaps it may be said, " We cordially assent to the
desirability of opening up China to Western civilisation; but we believe the civilian is better adapted to
accomplish that end than the soldier or sailor." To
this assertion I reply, that experience has shown the
fallacy of such a theory, and that the British man-of-
war has been the pioneer of progress in China. For
two hundred years we traded at Canton, and we knew
as much about China in 1830 as we did in 1630;
indeed, our merchants were worse treated at the ex-
piration of that time than at the commencement. It
was not until England appeared as a belligerent that
European civilisation progressed in the face of Chinese
exclusiveness. It was to the strong arm of the executive that Western nations were indebted for their extension of trade to the five ports, and for our increased
knowledge of that Empire; it was to the strong arm
of the executive—not to the diplomatist, and not to
the persuasions or enterprise of merchants or mission-
aries then resident in Canton—that Great Britain is indebted for her present revenue derivable from China.

There is a remarkable coincidence in our position
at this moment, and that at which the extension of
trade in China took place in 1840. I will give a brief
synopsis of the circumstances, for they cheer us with

the hope that now, as then, our sailors and soldiers will be the pioneers of extended commercial relations and extended knowledge of the Flowery Land.   In the year of grace 1839, we were forced into a war with China, not because they had slain or defeated her Majesty's forces, but because they compelled our agent to surrender to them a quantity of British property which they considered contraband.   There was then only one port of trade for us in all China : out of Canton came, in 150 ships, the 44 million pounds of tea then consumed by us.   It was an awful thing to contemplate the cutting off of such a supply ; the Chancellor of the Exchequer trembled for his customs receipts, and at first we vacillated, "kotowed," and submitted to every degradation rather than test the question, whether by incurring a little risk and a course worthy of Great Britain, we might not increase rather than diminish our trade with China.   Commissioner Lin of Canton was quite as much in the dark as to the commercial instincts of his countrymen and ours, as quidnuncs at home were.   He issued an edict, and stopped—as he fancied, poor man !—any more tea or rhubarb going to Britain, and wrote to Queen Victoria to tell her so.   The Emperor, through his delegate, used every effort to stop all our trade with China. Does any one remember tea being scarce, dearer than

usual, or worse than usual in consequence of those
Imperial efforts during the years 1840-41-42? I say,
not; for M'Culloch tells us that by 1844 the tea trade
of that port, in spite of a three years' war, had doubled
itself: in short, the Chinese merchants would trade in
spite of all hostilities, in spite of all edicts; and so
they ever have, and ever will do. The only apparent
difference in the trade was, that instead of our vessels
loading at Whampoa, they loaded about Lintin, or in
Hong-Kong and Macao. Yet remember—Lin and his
Emperor had placed us *hors-le-loi;* we were rebels—out-
casts—to be exterminated; and we had replied by a
counter-declaration of war: is it likely, therefore, that
if an Emperor of China, with China undisturbed by
rebellion, could not in 1840 at one port in his empire stop the trade with the English, that any exertion
upon his part would be able to effect such a result
at our five places of trade in 1860? Let Mr Gladstone
be at ease, therefore, upon that score, though at the
same time prepared for alarming telegrams of "no
more tea!—no more silk!" There will be about as
much real foundation in them as in those we receive
semi-monthly about those everlasting Taepings, and
that wondrous siege of Nankin, which appears to be
somehow mysteriously connected with the sales of
Chinese produce in Mincing Lane, and the secret of

which those who retail the strange compounds known
as tea in England can best explain.

But to my synopsis of the past. In 1840 our forces,
far too small for the task in hand, seized the Chusan
group of islands, and escorted our envoy to the mouth
of the Peiho. There was *one* vessel in all that force
that could cross the bar, and so far as being really in a
position to act against the capital of China, our admiral
and fleet might as well have hoped to operate against
Ispahan or Moscow. " Oh, you only want kind treat-
ment and an apology for past insults," said the mandarins of Taku. " Augh ! augh ! go back to Canton
again, give up Chusan when the apology arrives, and
all will be well." The unlucky envoy, unable to act,
hampered by instructions from home, fears of the
wrath of a Chancellor of the Exchequer, and beset by
the doubts of a mercantile *entourage,* came back to
Canton to find the apology an empty one, and that he
had been simply cajoled out of his hold on Chusan.

The year 1841 found us as far off any solution of
the question as 1839 had left us. Trade at Canton,
Hong-Kong, and Macao was, however, steadily increasing, contrary to the expectations of those ancients
supposed to be learned on Chinese matters ; and yet
there were not a few who deprecated farther prosecution of hostilities, not only on the score of humanity,
but on the advisability of letting well alone. Had they

—those humanitarians who denounced the opium war —been listened to, we should still have been trading with Canton Hong merchants, and known as much of China to-day as we did in the times of the Stuarts.

A more enlightened policy prevailed ; and in the summer of 1841 the naval and military authorities organised a force, and proceeded to act against the Chinese military forces on the coasts of Fokien and Chekiang provinces. We knew as much of these coasts then as we now do of those of Shantung and Pechelee—little or nothing. The forces explored and surveyed as they advanced. Wherever the authorities resisted us, they were firmly, but not inhumanly, expelled. The inhabitants of the great cities which fell into our hands saw that, though irresistible in combat, we were just and merciful ; and it is not too much to say that, quite apart from all question of military or naval glory, the able operations carried out in that autumn, winter, and following spring, were fraught with the utmost importance and benefit to China and Western civilisation generally.

Without those operations, the Treaty of Nankin, even if it ever had been signed, would not have been worth the paper upon which it was written.

Those military operations, those explorations of Fokien, Chekiang, and the Yang-tze-kiang up to the walls of Nankin, extended over a twelvemonth. The

whole military resources of the Empire were brought
against us. The Abbé Huc tells of the wild tribes of
Mongolia that were marched against us, and how the
Tartar horsemen, over their cups in those wild plains,
magnify their campaign against the fair-haired men
of the sea; and we know that even the untamed
Meaoutsze of the Himalayan ranges were brought
down to exterminate those who would intrude upon
the privacy of the Flowery Land. The Emperor and
Court did all that was in their power to bring upon
us the whole weight of the masses, and they utterly
failed.

The Chinaman would trade : he did so, in the captured cities, before the mandarin who died in resisting
us at its gates was buried. The Chinese merchant of
Ningpo hired us vehicles, sold us stores, wherewith
to master the mandarin ; and in the self-same day
obtained a ball-and-peacock-feather decoration for a
voluntary contribution to his own government towards
exterminating us. He was only a Chinaman—a creature who looked to profit, and left conscience for priests
and women to babble of.

And what did they do at Canton during all those
twelvemonths that we were warring in Central China?
—simply traded. The mandarins might look sulky ;
patriotic retired officials, and Hong merchants who had
made their fortunes by the past condition of foreign

commerce, might have been alarmed lest the vested
interests of Canton in foreign trade should be impaired
by the new order of things which then only loomed in
the distance, and the provincial government, urged by
the Court to do something against the barbarian,
might have threatened, but all wisely satisfied themselves with pouring stones into the channels of the
Pearl River, in order that their odorous city of Canton might never again be harassed by the presence
of British men-of-war. Trade still went on, openly
or covertly, for the native authorities soon discovered that to forbid commercial transactions with
the foreigner was simply to sacrifice their revenue
derivable from it, without depriving us of our tea and
silks.

The Cantonese were not sorry to see transferred to
other quarters the punishment which their insolence
and bigotry had brought down upon the Government ;
and having themselves reported the English to be
" uncontrollable and fierce," they did not regret to find
that the inhabitants of Fokien and Chekiang province
were likely to come to the same conclusion. There
was something truly Chinese in the sly chuckle with
which your Canton friend described the astonishment
and terror of the mandarins in Amoy and Chin-hae at
the advent of Sir Hugh Gough and the 18th Royal
Irish ; and no one would have had to go farther than

Hog Lane, or " Old Curiosity Street," in Canton, to
become a firm believer in the truth of Rochefoucault's
assertion, that " dans l'adversité de nos meilleurs amis,
nous trouvons toujours quelque chose qui ne nous
déplaît pas."

I have dwelt rather longer than I intended upon
this retrospect, but my object is to meet the objections
made to a declaration of war or warlike operations in
China, lest trade at the open ports should be stopped,
or lest the population—the masses—should rise against
us.   We may even point to the experience of 1857-58
to prove that in China such a thing is unheard of, as
that whilst you are carrying on successful military
operations in one province, the Chinamen dwelling in
another one should be guilty of running their heads
against the victor.   It would be quite contrary to Li
or reason.   Whilst the battles of Canton and Fatshan
were being fought with Commissioner Yeh in Quang-
tung, trade was flourishing at Amoy, Foo-chow, and
and Shanghai.   Whilst the Allies were blowing up the
Taku earthworks, and marching about Tientsin, in
1858 ; whilst the alarmed Court were signing treaties,
and decapitating those officers who failed to repel us
in our approach to Pekin,—all went pleasant as a
marriage-bell in Shanghai, and would have done so in
Canton likewise, but that we had touched the *amour
propre* of the natives of that province by forcing a

garrison of British troops upon them, and they retaliated by hostile demonstrations of a purely local character. Where there is no chivalry, no generosity, in the heart of a people, there cannot be, I maintain, that patriotism which will lead them to blindly support a weak Government against a strong assailant. The Government of Pekin, it is true, can raise contributions of men or money in all the provinces of the Empire; we have experienced this, and we know its extent already; but a levy *en masse*—a general wish to thrust us forth at any sacrifice, personal or pecuniary—is not in the disposition of the people, or in the power of its effete Government.

Monsieur Huc, who has lived more amongst Chinamen, and knows them better, than perhaps any of our countrymen, confirms so much my opinions of the want of a generous or chivalrous feeling in the Chinese, that I must give his words:—" At Manilla," says Huc, " the number of Chinese Christians is considerable; but that may be ascribed to the effect of a law passed by the Spaniards, which forbids a Chinese to marry a native woman until he has become a Christian. When the Chinese wish to marry, therefore, they receive baptism just as they would go through any other ceremony that was required. But if, even after the lapse of many years, the fancy takes them to return to their own country, *they leave the wife and religion behind,*

and go back as they came. It is this radical, profound
indifference to all religion—an indifference that is
scarcely conceivable by any who have not witnessed it
—which is, in our opinion, the real grand obstacle that
has so long opposed the progress of Christianity in
China. The Chinese is so completely absorbed in
temporal interests, in the things which fall under his
senses, that his whole life is only materialism put in
action. Lucre is the sole object on which his eyes are
constantly fixed. A burning thirst to realise some
profit, great or small, absorbs all his faculties—the
whole energy of his being. He never pursues anything with ardour but riches and material enjoyments."
With such a people—and I believe the picture drawn
by Huc to be a perfect photograph of the race—we
need not fear that they will throw themselves as one
man between us and their Emperor, or that they will
allow a lucrative trade to be interfered with, because
he chooses to encourage a Manchou general, who is at
the head of the reactionary party in the Pekinese
cabinet, in an act of treachery towards us.

With respect to the lasting impression left upon the
minds of the inhabitants of those portions of China
where we first appear as belligerents, not as traders
simply, and of the salutary influence such an impression ever after exercises in our favour, we need do
little more than point to our relations since 1842 with

the native officials and residents of Amoy, Ningpo,
Chusan, and Shanghai. Every merchant and consul
in China will, I feel sure, bear me out in saying that
the effect there has been most salutary through a long
course of seventeen years, and in marked contrast to
what is experienced at Canton.

At Canton I hold that much of the contempt for us
arises from our having hesitated, in 1840, to convince
them of the superiority of our military power, by
accepting a ransom of six million dollars instead of
marching through that city—an error subsequently
redeemed at the sacrifice of more English treasure and
more English lives than I should like the honourable
Member for Lambeth to be fully aware of.

By force of arms we opened five ports of China to
European intercourse in 1842. So far did our knowledge of that country increase, and no farther ; for
we have but to peruse the writings, blue-books, and
pamphlets upon China between 1842 and 1857, to be
convinced how little progress the European com-
munities at the five ports had made during that period,
in opening up to the knowledge of Europe that vast
hive of human beings, at whose threshold they were
simply tolerated.

When the Treaty of Nankin was signed in 1842, and
our fleet withdrawn, sanguine people—who did not
understand the stolidity of the Chinaman, and who did

not appreciate the extent of his country, and the barriers, moral and physical, which prevented a peaceful opening up of China—dreamed that from those five ports would go forth a spirit of religious and commercial enterprise which would, before long, had their views been realised, have made it an Eden teeming with pious free-traders. Nothing of the sort has taken place; the old Jesuit map of China, compiled two centuries ago, is still our only guide, not only for all the interior, but even for those provinces on the seaboard of which our civilians have been so long located.*

Our naval surveyors, Captains Kellett and Collinson, it is true, surveyed the coast between Shanghai and Canton; but when hostilities commenced in 1857, *beyond the points attained by our soldiers and sailors, our belligerents, in* 1842, *there was no local information whatever;* and it was only during the prosecution of recent hostilities that the explorations of the Peiho River to Tientsin, of the Yang-tze to Hankow, and of the West River in Quang-tung province, were either practicable, or have been accomplished. When, in November 1858, I wanted information about the Yang-tze-kiang prior to my ascent in H.M.S. Furious

* We believe that this curious and antiquated piece of topography has just been reproduced for the use of our naval and military authorities in China by the topographical department of the War Office. Of course, in the absence of any better, our officials could not do otherwise.

to Hankow, there was not a soul in Shanghai, whether
consul, missionary, or merchant, who knew one fresh
fact connected with that stream or of the lands and
people beyond it, beyond the point to which the fleet,
under Admiral Sir William Parker, reached in 1842 ;
yet they had been fifteen years living almost upon the
banks of that great artery of China! In Canton it
was still more strange ; the West River was known to
flow from Western Quang-tung, and to join the Canton
River near Macao. Yet, when Commodore M'Cleverty
started to ascend it with an armed expedition in the
spring of 1859, he was going upon quite as explora-
tory an expedition as if he had been in search of the
sources of the Nile, or the Arctic Polynia. Europeans
had been 240 years at the entrance of the West River,
yet knew not whether, or how far, it was navigable.
The causes of this want of increase of knowledge of
China during peace time, I have nothing to do with ;
I merely point out the fact. It is a homely simile,
but not less true on that account, that China is an
oyster, which must and will only open to our good
swords and strong wills.

Before passing to the consideration of the best means
by which this may be effected, I deprecate any idea of
it being supposed that, because there are fourteen out
of the eighteen provinces of China with which we have
no relations, that I deem it possible they should all be

I

at once *exploité*; or, secondly, that I desire to dictate precisely to our military or naval authorities what their course of action should be.

I will, in the first place, strive to show the resources of the untouched portions of the Chinese Empire, and to point out those places or provinces immediately accessible to us; whence, in good time, farther progress may eventually be made. I am no believer in finality; and leave that faith to the gentlemen of the Foreign Office. I hold the Treaty of Tientsin to be a very good one, but God forbid that I should say that a better one for British interests may not be required within the next fifteen or twenty years. What a blessing fifteen years of perfect peace with China will be, reader!—prithee do not smile and under-estimate its value; if you do, read and ponder over the history of our last fourteen years' intercourse with that country, and you will then assuredly say with me, if that is Peace, in the name of all that is merciful, let us have war for twelve months, provided it inaugurate a healthier condition of our commercial and political relations!

In the first place, if the finger be run up the sea-coast of a map of China, which is about two thousand miles in extent from the Gulf of Tonquin to the head of that of Leo-tong, it will be found that we have as yet only had access or trade with exactly one-half of

that extent of coast—viz. the provinces of Quang-tung,
Fokien, and Chekiang, and a portion of Kiang-soo,
leaving two-thirds of Kiang-soo, all Shantung, Pecheli,
and Shingking, totally without a seaport open to our
traders or our ships ; and it is therefore apparent that,
in sending our sailors to explore those provinces, we
shall not interfere in any way with the portion of the
sea-coast to which our merchant ships now go and
come.

The next consideration is, are those provinces likely
to yield a profitable trade, and in what way will they
affect our future relations with the Empire of China?
Happily, although we possess no perfect chart of the
regions in question, it so happens that the information brought by our two embassies to the capital,
and the partial explorations of 1858, compared with
Chinese statistical and geographical information collected by our Sinologues from Chinese gazetteers, leave
but little doubt upon this point. We find, that whereas
the combined population of the three sea-coast provinces we are trading with, represents the total figure
of sixty millions, that of the untouched provinces of
the northern sea-coast equals fifty-nine millions,[*]
without taking into consideration any portion of the
thirty-eight million souls who dwell in Kiang-soo, the
rich delta of the Yang-tze and Hoang-ho.

[*] See Chinese Census for 1812. .

Furthermore; if we consider our open ports in
Southern China the gateways by which the streams
of civilisation and commerce are to permeate through
the provinces immediately contiguous and bordering
upon them : it will be found that, whereas that region,
south of the great river which cuts China in twain,
contains one hundred and thirty-six millions of Chinese,
the northern half of the Empire—that is, Northern
China with which we have as yet had no commercial
relations—boasts of two hundred and twenty-six millions ; and knowing, as we do, that every Chinaman
is equally industrious, what a vision of our future trade
does it conjure up, when we know there is such a field
lying fallow to the trader and manufacturer of England !

There is one essential difference, too, between Northern and Southern China, which must ever be borne
in mind : the south is the producing, almost tropical
region, whose exports must ever be in excess of imports,
for the soil teems with vegetable products, and the
climate is so genial that the Chinaman's wants are few.
In the north, on the contrary, we have over half of its
area the climate and products of the temperate zone,
and much of it will be found an importing rather than
an exporting country, the wealth of the provinces in
metals, wools, oil, seed, timber, wheat, and pulse, en-
abling them to pay handsomely for the luxuries and
necessaries they will soon learn to purchase from Eng-

land. Man must not only labour there, and does so
with all the innate love of industry, that thirst for
gain which marks the race ; but he cannot, after having won competence, gamble it away in naked inde-
pendence, under the open sky, as they do in the south
of China—the climate is far too severe for that. In
all the densely inhabited provinces of Northern China,
people must be housed, clothed, and comfortably fed,
or they perish in the winter. Commerce—the interchange of what they have for what they have not—
must be as much a necessity with the inhabitants of
Pecheli and Shantung, as it is a taste or habit with
those of Quang-tung.

One of the most wealthy and influential native commercial guilds with which our people have come in
contact in China has relations with this northern region,
and is known as the "Shantung Guild, or Hong."
Its wealth and importance are thoroughly recognised;
and, apart from the major portion of the coasting trade
of Northern China being in its hands, its vessels or
junks are found at Singapore, Batavia, and Siam. This
guild was one of the first to memorialise against the
concessions connected with the trade in the north made
to the English at Tientsin—a trade in which there was
every reason to believe the Shantung Hong transactions
and profits to be enormous—and there is no doubt
that they have good grounds for dreading our arrival

in the profitable field, which exists in supplying the
bare wants of the populations round the Gulf of
Pecheli.

That the necessity for trade there must be great,
and that the Chinamen of the north will make any
effort rather than forego it, we have a very remarkable
example in the recent history of the grain trade to the
capital. For centuries all that grain had been transported by a particular route, that of the Great Canal,
in frail river vessels, for which boatmen rather than
seamen were necessary. Suddenly, when the exigency
occurred, that trade was turned into another remote,
dangerous, and difficult channel ; but they mastered all
obstacles, and showed themselves anything but anti-
progressive when compelled to be so.

However, before we enter upon the nature and extent
of that grain trade, which is of a purely import character, let me point to the recognised products of Shantung, Pecheli, and Shingking provinces, as a means to
pay for their wants.

Shantung has several harbours, and produces wheat,
maize, millet, enough for its own consumption, and
occasionally for export. Coal, timber, and iron abound.
Cattle, and animals such as the horse, donkey, and
mule, are more plentiful than in the south, and it is
famous for the abundance and excellence of its vegetables and fruits, which resemble those of Europe.

Shantung monopolises all the Corean trade, and it will be from Shantung that the European will have to lay siege to the exclusive system prevailing in the Corea over fifteen millions of people, dwelling in a remarkably fine country.

Of the resources of Pecheli we know less than of its wants ; but from what our embassies and our sailors have seen of it, the major portion appears to be a steppe country, intersected with a few rivers, but abounding in vast salines, from which the Government extracts a great deal of salt, and it retails as a mono-poly and important source of revenue. Sheep, and consequently wool, must be abundant ; but its prin-cipal wealth consists in coals, minerals, and clay for porcelain. Nitre is so plentiful here that saltpetre would in all probability form, under our auspices, an important article of commerce.

Beyond Pecheli and west of it, lies the extensive province of Shansi. This, the ancient seat of the Chinese race, is an important and desirable region for us to obtain access to. Fourteen millions of people dwell there in a rich but mountainous region, where the climate compels them to clothe themselves warmly, and whither they find it worth while to drag and carry the woollen manufactures of Moscow across Siberia and Mongolia,—a terrible land journey of many thou-sand miles!—yet we at Tientsin city, where men of

war of 800 tons burden have reached, can put them
down the good broadcloth of Leeds, at a much lower
figure, and only give them a transit of 120 miles to
their homes.   The native writers speak highly of the
resources of Shansi, and upon their authority we are
told in the *Chinese Repository* that "it exhibits great
diversity in its animal, vegetable, and mineral products,
and the principal source of wealth of the inhabitants
lies in its mines of coal, iron, cinnabar, copper, marble,
lapis-lazuli, salt, and precious stones, as well as metals."
This province forms, as it were, the eastern slopes of
the high table-lands of Central Asia, where they sink
into the plains of Pecheli; and, as I have already
pointed out, our most direct route to it for the present,
to insure as short a land-carriage as possible, is directly
across the province of Pecheli; the river Peiho, the
When-ho, and other streams facilitating our transit
very considerably.

We now come to Shingking, at the head of the
Gulf of Pecheli.   This province, although at the first
glance it may not appear so, is, I feel assured, likely
before very long to take an important position, com-
mercially and politically speaking, in Eastern Asia.   It
is the outlet of all Manchouria : its sea-port, Neu-
chang, lies now only 600 miles from the Russian
frontier, and that frontier will probably, before next
Christmas, be even nearer to the waters of the Yellow

Sea. Manchouria, though said to be thinly populated, is a great pastoral region, producing vast quantities of that precious golden fleece which we find it worth while to coax to our marts down the passes of the Himalaya and Hindoo-koosh, and to carry in our ships from Australia or Peru. The province of Shingking is said to have a severe climate, but it produces and exports, as the shores of the Baltic do in spite of sharp winters, vast quantities of cereals, pulse, and oil-seeds. Russian Siberia will before long—possibly in our day —play an important part in the history of the Asiatic continent, and is only accessible to us through the sea-port of Neu-chang, and thence by Moukden and Kirin to that grand curve in the Amour river whither General Mouravieff and his able coadjutor, Admiral Count Putiatin, cleverly carried forward their boundary-line in 1858.

Lofty and inhospitable mountain-ranges bar out Man-chouria from the Sea of Japan, and northward of that no Europeans are likely to go for commercial purposes in our merchant ships. What Kurrachee is with respect to Beloochistan, Afghanistan, and Bokhara, the port of Neu-chang will one day be to the great region of Man-chouria and Eastern Tartary. Whenever Siberia seeks a direct communication with the Tropical regions of Asia, and a facile route to China or India, she will strike for the head of the Gulf of Pecheli, from her

present frontier on the Amoor. For political as well
as commercial reasons we ought to be there, and, D.V.,
shall be there before her. It reflects great credit upon
Lord Elgin that he should have looked so much to the
future in obtaining this important place, Neu-chang,
as one of the future seaports open to European commerce ; and we may hope he will secure to us there, as
we possess elsewhere in China, the privilege of carrying
the produce of the country to and from its own ports
in British vessels—an application of free-trade principles in coasting-trade, which has proved already most
beneficial to the English shipowners in China, and to
which we cordially call the attention of our American
cousins ; for, strange to say, the Emperor and Court
of Pekin have outstripped the President and Senate
of Washington in enlightenment upon the navigation
laws.

Such are the commercial prospects involved in the
region immediately accessible to us. I must now
crave the reader's attention to the history of the grain
trade between Southern China and the province of
Pecheli, because much misapprehension exists in England as to its present extent or importance, as well as
of the mode in which it passes in to the northward.
It was by cutting off this much-needed supply of food
for the capital, as well as by those military operations
to which I have already alluded, that our Admiral and

General in 1842 succeeded in placing Sir Henry Pottinger in a position to dictate the Treaty of Nankin;
and although an exact repetition of their advance on
that southern capital would be totally inefficacious in
1860, still the general spirit of their strategy might
very safely be followed.

The history and statistics of the grain trade with
Southern China, though it be almost what we should
term a Government monopoly, gives us, apart from its
commercial bearings, a great insight into the condition
of the population of Pecheli, and of the position of
dependence of the Court upon a supply which energy
upon our part will enable us to intercept. Thanks to
the labours and researches of that learned Chinese
scholar, Mr Thomas Wade,* Secretary to the British

* This gentleman's valuable and unrequited services to his country
are a sad commentary upon the encouragements given by Government
to persons of education who will devote their abilities to acquiring a
language so difficult to thoroughly master as that of China. Originally an officer in the gallant corps commanded in China by Lord Clyde,
then Colonel Colin Campbell, Mr Wade turned a close attention to the
Chinese language and literature; he then entered our Consular service,
and has ever since been labouring in the higher branches of an interpreter's duties. Deeply read in all the writings of China, a thorough
master of the Pekinese dialect, such a man would, in France or Russia,
be decorated, and held up for all men to admire. Without such as
him, Ambassadors, Generals, and Admirals would be perfectly help-
less in China; yet we, who have at last learnt to appreciate energetic
commissaries, good doctors, and conscientious chaplains, can find
nothing to reward or decorate the ablest Chinese scholar of our day!
No! we shall simply work him to death; or, if he lives, give him a
Civil Service superannuation!

Legation, we are enabled to place before the English
public a mass of information upon the grain trade
of Northern China, the magnitude of which promises
well for our Indian possessions, especially those of
Tenasserim and Bengal. We can thence send from
our superabundant harvests any quantity of food
to the inhabitants of Shantung and Pecheli, and
place the tonnage of shipping employed in that import trade at the disposal of our English merchants
in China for their Chinese exports of tea and silk—
a much more convenient mode, so far as England
is concerned, of furnishing them with tonnage at
low rates, than a petty war with China, in which
we pay high for freights of coals and munitions of
war to Hong-Kong, and the trader hires the empty
transports at a very low rate to send his investments
home.

It appears, according to the statistics of the Pekin
Board of Revenue, as well as various official documents which have appeared in Pekin Gazettes dating
as late as 1856, that the quantity of rice necessary
for annual consumption in the capital amounted to the
enormous sum of 430,000 tons; and this agrees with
a statistical report for 1831, in which the rule is
pointed out that there should always be in store, in
Pekin, 354,000 tons of rice, and at Tung-chow, a city
upon the banks of the Peiho River, above Tientsin,

and only twelve miles distant from Pekin, another
reserve of 80,000 tons.

The whole of this vast quantity of food is the proceeds of the land-tax, or tribute to the Crown, as
owner of the soil. In five of the provinces the tithe
is commuted, producing an annual sum of 246,570
ounces of silver; the rest of China supplies grain and
pulse in the following proportions:—Common rice,
210,000 tons; fine rice for the Court, 44,000 tons;
wheat, 4000 tons; pulse, 17,000 tons. All the wheat
and pulse is grown in Shantung, the adjacent province of Honan, and in that Manchouria of which
people have hitherto had so ill an opinion. The
annual collection of grain commences in the first week
of November, and within two months—that is, early
in January—all grain so collected had to be shipped
off to the Grand Canal, by means of the rivers or
streams which led towards it. This canal was the
artery by which the capital was fed, and great system
was necessary to prevent confusion amongst the vast
number of vessels employed. A high officer used to
superintend this transport duty, having under him
no less than 64,000 men embarked in 6318 junks,
divided into 123 squadrons.

He dwelt at an important city called Hwai-gan-fou,
on the south bank of the Hoang-Ho, or Yellow River,
just at the intersection of the Grand Canal, and thence

he annually despatched the grain northward in three fleets—the first fleet commencing the ascent of the canal from the Yellow River to Tientsin in January and February; the second fleet in March; the third in April. Each fleet occupied about twelve weeks, or rather that was the time given by the regulations of the service for the voyage from the Yellow River to Tientsin on the Peiho River.

At Tientsin the grain was put into barges, and carried to Tung-chow, and thence conveyed in carts to the granaries of Pekin. Such was the mode in which the capital was supplied when the British fleet, in 1842, ascended the Yang-tze-Kiang, and intercepted the Grand Canal where it connects that stream with the Yellow River. The alarm occasioned by the threatened stoppage of the supplies of grain from the provinces of Southern China, doubtless did much to bring the capital and Court to its senses. But inasmuch as famine had been no novelty at Pekin prior to that year 1842, we believe that the terror inspired by the success of our military operations at Shanghai, Woosung, and Chin-kiang-foo, conducted still more to bring about the supplication for peace which followed the arrival of our forces off Nankin.

In 1850, the *Pekin Gazette* contained a memorial from one of the senior Court Censors, named Wang-tung-hwai, calling attention, amongst other things, to the necessity of looking to the supplies then in the grain magazines of the capital, and he urged the Emperor to see that extraordinary efforts were made to hasten in from the adjacent provinces about 170,725 tons of grain said to be available, otherwise, the Censor remarks, there will only be " enough grain (in 1851) to last some months."

It is to be hoped that this was done, for in 1851 a terrible calamity occurred. The Yellow River, a constant source of anxiety to the authorities charged with the preservation of its embankments, burst out violently in a northerly direction over the works constructed for the maintenance of the Grand Canal, and injured one of the most important reservoirs, a sort of artificial lake, which supplied the water for the canal at the higher levels in Shantung province; and consequently, when the last grain fleets in 1852 tried to reach Tientsin, they utterly failed, and the grain had to be transported overland from the borders of Shantung. The distress in the north became very great; and in 1853, acted upon by the impracticable condition of the canal, and the fear of the rebellion then rapidly spreading, another Censor urged the *transport of grain by sea*. It is worthy of notice that he likewise accepts the quantity required as about 430,000 tons of grain: and in that autumn 333 junks, laden with grain, reached the Gulf of Pecheli in safety.

Such was the recommencement of the sea-trade in grain, which China had abandoned many centuries before, in consequence, it is said, of the risks and uncertainties attendant upon its transport, arising from the prevalence of piracy, and from the boisterous weather of the Yellow sea and Gulf of Pecheli.

In 1854, the sea-borne grain trade saved the Emperor and Court from capitulating to the Taeping hordes, who, having swept down the Yang-tze River from the Poyang Lake to Nankin, and established themselves in that city, had boldly advanced northward by the direct route which the now neglected and damaged Grand Canal afforded. The loyal authorities of Southern China, especially from the province of Chekiang, despatched 100,000 tons of rice by sea to Tientsin; and whilst the Manchoo forces under Prince Sung-o-losin * beat back the Taepings, all that grain was carried in 3892 river junks to Tung-chow, between the dates of June 7th and August 3d—a remarkable proof of the river transport available to our forces in that same neighbourhood, to which we call the attention of our military and naval authorities; and we trust it will relieve the minds of those alarmists who fancy there are insuperable difficulties in the transport of the *materiel* of

---

* This is the same redoubtable individual who subsequently conducted the treacherous attack upon Admiral Hope's flotilla in 1859.

our forces towards Pekin—Tung-chow being but twelve miles from the capital.

In May 1856, says our informant, the Governor of Chekiang, in a somewhat self-complacent memorial, reported the shipment from his province of about 60,000 tons of grain in 721 junks; and mentioned that it was four years since the sea-transport of rice was commenced, and that it is yearly increasing. We learn likewise, that by 5th July, 1200 junks had discharged 100,000 tons of grain at Tientsin and returned south, and that 6000 tons were still at sea, and due there. In this year, the Taeping rebels having withdrawn to their stronghold of Nankin, the canal was again surveyed, but reported to have sustained irreparable injury between Shantung and the Yellow river. Whether it was that the rice crops generally failed in the south, or that the authorities there did not sufficiently exert themselves to victual the capital during the summer of 1856, is uncertain, but famine raged in Pekin that winter—a conclusive proof that the 100,000 tons delivered from Chekiang, as well as what came from Manchouria and Shantung, was insufficient for the wants of the capital.

In 1857 the authorities appear to have determined to abandon the Grand Canal route for the Imperial grain fleet. The Board of Revenue proposed to dispose of the canal junks, and some of the more remote and western provinces of the Empire were called upon to pay their land-tax in coin instead of grain. In 1858, when our forces threw themselves into the Peiho, and occupied Tientsin, the river was found to be positively crammed with grain junks from all parts of the sea-coast of the Empire; and the number of those peculiar to the adjacent sea-board of Manchouria went far to support a report published in the *Gazette* for 1857, that as much as 3000 tons of grain had been paid that year as tribute or tax from Shingking.

During the allied occupation of Tientsin, the price of rice there in the shops was about twice what it was at Shanghai; and knowing that our merchants had found it worth while to import into Shanghai in 1857 no less than 54,000 tons at Shanghai prices, we can easily fancy how much more satisfactory it would be to them to have the supplying of all the hungry mouths of the province of Pecheli. The Chinese authorities are, however, fully alive to the inconvenience of leaving their supplies of food at the mercy of a foreigner, the dreaded " outside barbarian "—and knowing what a narrow escape they had of the whole grain fleet of 1858 being intercepted, it is by no means unlikely that they will make, or have made, great efforts *to again convey a portion of the grain to Pekin by way of the canal.* My attention has been more directly called to this point, in consequence of private letters from

Shanghai, informing me that the Imperial authorities at the city of Chin-kiang-foo (which commands the mouth of the Grand Canal) are busy erecting batteries on Silver Island in the Yang-tze River, as if to prevent our approach to the canal. There can be no difficulty in repairing all the southern portion of the canal—that is, from Hwang-chow-foo up to the south bank of the Yellow River—and possibly, aided by as good engineers as those who taught them to construct the Taku forts of 1859, the Chinese, if they cannot render the northern half of their great internal artery perfectly navigable, may so reduce the impediments as to necessitate but a very short land-transport, and thus place the canal in a condition to become a very important auxiliary in furnishing the capital, if we should simply attempt a coast blockade, with the hope of starving the Court into its senses.

Such is the history of this grain trade; and I do not think I have magnified its importance, when it is remembered that a series of military operations, which shall re-establish our military prestige, and at the same time insure a perfect stoppage of that supply, must starve a capital of some two million souls into subjection; whilst the value of that grain represents in coin a sum which will defray us for the war. Moreover, any arrangement which shall give Europeans the power of sharing directly in that grain trade, will not only be a great benefit to our shipowners and merchants, but also place in our hands the bridle with which to check in future the pugnacity or impertinence of the Emperor and Court.

I am aware that it will be said, " But this grain is a simple tax, on its way to the Imperial exchequer. How can we, in time of peace, have anything to do with it?" I reply, In two ways. First, Insist upon the right to import grain into Tientsin, as we now do into Canton and Shanghai; we shall find a great market for it, and whenever, through drought, rebellion, or other causes, the Chinese harvests fail, the Government of Pekin will look to us to arrest famine, and we shall be able to do it for them. Secondly, Insist upon the same privileges in the coasting trade of Northern China as all Europeans enjoy in Southern China. I know, from the best authority, that cargoes of Indian and Batavian rice are now bought from us in Shanghai, and shipped off to Teintsin in junks. Let us, I say, deliver that rice in British bottoms, or, if they like, carry their own tribute rice there instead.

We will now pass to the probable course of military operations in China, our main object being, we presume, to bring the Court to its senses as rapidly as possible, to open up the unknown region called Northern China—to explore it, in fact—and at the same time to secure such an indemnity as will lighten, if not entirely relieve us from the expenses of a great military expedition.

In the first place, we cannot now, it is very certain, withdraw the garrison from Canton. Three or four thousand soldiers and half-a-dozen vessels will have to hold it, and keep the communications open with Hong-Kong: for this service a portion of the native troops we are sending from India will be probably employed, replacing the melancholy remnant of the two magnificent battalions of Marines, and one wing of H.M. Royal Regiment, which disease may have spared. Hong-Kong with its 80,000 Chinese inhabitants and 170 English ones, with its naval dockyard, factory, commissariat stores, and millions of British property, will require at least another thousand men, and a large man-of-war with a couple of gun-boats. Swatow and Amoy will each call for a man-of-war to protect our merchants, and Foo-chow, as well as Ningpo, will need similar support, simply to prevent the mandarins, at the instigation of their Government, issuing edicts which may alarm the traders, native or foreign. Shanghai, which in commercial importance ranks equal to Canton, will require the constant presence of a large vessel capable of landing a respectable force, should the safety of the foreign property in the warehouses be threatened.

In simple precautionary measures, five thousand bayonets and twelve vessels of war will be probably required at the five ports and Hong-Kong. This force would doubtless maintain the peace; but with a Chinaman, as with all Asiatics, the worse strategy is to be on the defensive; he immediately fancies you are afraid of him, and every petty mandarin seeks to secure imperial favour and honour by harassing and insulting the foreigner, alarming the merchants, and carrying on a series of petty hostilities. Of course he could not do this without funds, but unfortunately we are actually supplying them with the means of thus annoying us, in the payment of the fiscal dues upon our exports and imports, a portion of which every Prefect at the open ports can apply to an exhibition of local patriotism, whilst he remits the major portion to the capital, for the extirpation of the barbarian, who has thus been good enough to supply powder and shot for his own slaughter! Now, in order to check these official patriots, we would suggest, that at each seaport the reasoning faculty of the Chinese authorities be appealed to, and that they be informed that, although we will rigidly pay all lawful custom-dues into the custom-houses, the sum accruing must be placed in the hands of joint trustees, to await the decision of the Imperial and allied authorities at the conclusion of peace.

When Shanghai was in the hands of the rebels some few years since, and it seemed doubtful whether we should shortly have to pay custom-dues to the present dynasty or to the new one represented by some Taeping worthy, who blasphemously claimed relationship with the Christian Trinity, the custom-dues were temporarily sequestrated, though trade went on ; and the Chinese Imperial authorities, finding there was little choice in the matter, allowed that such a course was conformable to the " divine principles of reason." We have little doubt that a notice, firm but civil, to the like effect, would not create much dissatisfaction at the five ports, although the Emperor Hien-fung and General Sung-o-losin might curl their mustaches with ire, and urge a speedy slaughter of the red-haired ones under Admiral Hope and Sir H. Grant.

Such a measure, apart from crippling those sinews of war, which are as essential in China as in Europe, would give us within a twelvemonth no very despicable sum of dollars, which might be claimed for indemnity. The returns to the Chinese treasury from the custom-dues of Shanghai alone, where the new system of collecting is thoroughly established, equal nearly a million pounds sterling ; indeed, in 1859, I find that Europeans paid at that port alone, in dues upon imports and exports, 3,932,378 taels of silver, each tael equal to 6s. 8d., or a grand total of £1,310,792 sterling ! and this does not include very heavy port dues upon 1865 European vessels which cleared during the same period, neither does it include the new rate of a pound sterling import-tax on every chest of opium—and they were reported at 32,102 chests. The Canton dues ought to be about as much more, and the rest of the other ports should yield another million : in fact, there is little doubt that about three millions sterling could thus be easily available within the coming year. No very alarming sum either in the shape of a tax, when we are told that, during the past year, the European imports and exports into Shanghai, amounted to the extraordinary value in figures of £28,454,975 sterling, and that the able Comptroller-General of Foreign Customs there says he believes that sum to be considerably under the real value of the trade in that port! Indeed, from a rough but careful computation, the entire European and Indian trade with China cannot be less than 100 millions sterling !

The figures I have given of the Shanghai custom-dues are official—there can be no error in them. I do not deny the right of the Imperial Government of China to these dues in peace time ; and although mandarins and Emperor may curl their noses in disdain at such paltry sums, when we strive to make them allow the importance of foreign trade to the Celestial Exchequer, it does appear cruel and unjust that such sums, which in the long run come out of our pockets in England, should be devoted by a Chinaman to the purchase of powder

and guns wherewith to resist the just demands of
Great Britain ; and it does seem only fair and politic
that the dues arising from the trade with Europeans
should go to indemnify Europeans for the expense they
are being put to in making the Court of Pekin adhere
to its engagements.

The next measure I would suggest is, that proclama-
tions be made along the coast from Hainan Island to the
Yang-tze-kiang ; that in the event of any town or district moving on behalf of the capital by extraordinary
contributions of money or munitions of war, it should
be visited with hostilities ; that a heavy tax or ransom
should be levied, and that its native trade in junks
should have immediately inflicted upon it a war-tax of
10 per cent *ad valorem.* This measure was adopted in
1841-42, when the native monopolists of Chekiang
province contributed towards expelling us from Ningpo
and Chusan, and the result was most beneficial to the
English military-chests, and salutary in its effect upon
the gentry, who perhaps did not regret a measure
which justified them in the eyes of their own authorities for lukewarmness in patriotism.

Any one who has visited the coasts, or read of the
vast coasting-trade of China, can fancy what a tax
levied upon it would produce ; and although it is to be
hoped that the acts of the seaboard population in Quan-
tung, Fokien, and Chekiang may not render such a

measure necessary, still I know of no better pre-
ventive for any hostility upon the part of a Chinaman,
than a knowledge that it would result in a pecuniary
mulct.

Having thus secured the interruption of one of the
most valuable feeders of the Imperial treasury ; provided a means of indemnification which would not press
upon those inhabitants of China who are innocent of
this war ; and suspended a rod over the heads of the
authorities in China, our forces will then be free to act
upon those points most likely to have an effect upon
Emperor and Court ; and where military operations
can in no way effect our trade, inasmuch as we have no
trade in those ports.   Our latest information proves,
as I anticipated when these remarks originally appeared
in *Blackwood*, that we were too late to do anything before the heats of the Pekin summer set in.   The allied
expedition, a wonderfully large one to be sent so far
for a simple apology as we have been told, had not
all left Hong-Kong in the middle of May.   However,
they were progressing, and establishing depots, hospitals, and other necessary *points d'appui* as they advanced.   The Chusan group has wisely been occupied ;
as a strategical point, it is of infinite importance ; and
on its breezy hills our fever and dysentery-stricken
countrymen will recover, doubtless, that health and
strength wasted so rapidly in the plains of Continental

China. The beautiful island of Pootoo is to be our
sanatarium, and it has especial advantages which must
render our having selected it a subject of congratula-
tion to all who have friends and relatives in the Chinese
expedition. Between it and Japan, we may confidently
trust that the frightful mortality which has hitherto
rendered China so sadly notorious amongst soldiers and
sailors, may be considerably checked. The Allies, as
they assemble in the Chusan group, and at the entrance
of the Yang-tze, will find the climate in June unpleasantly hot. All will hasten on northward for
Shantung, where, though the days be hot, and the
July winds loaded with the sand and soil of the plains
of Pecheli and of the desert beyond, the nights, nevertheless, are cool and refreshing. To the ports of Shantung the commissaries will have already preceded the
fleets, and thence will be directed all the supplies which,
we hear, the foresight of the naval Commander-in-
Chief and the Commissary-general has already sought
from the Eastern Archipelago, from Australia, Java,
and the East Indies. Everybody will long to be in and
doing in the north ; we can sympathise for those whose
fate it will be to remain chained up at the five ports as
watch-dogs for English interests ; and we can feel for
those who will have to look to the important but in-
glorious details of furnishing all the supplies, and for-
warding them safely in the wake of the impatient host

who are going to open Northern China. We can fancy
the frantic efforts that Chinese diplomacy will then
make to gain time, to delay until winter sets in and
paralyses our forces, and nothing that chicanery and
Eastern duplicity are capable of will fail to be exer-
cised ; but it is then that we trust the firmness of our
Ambassador will shine forth, and that he will say,
" We want the Treaty of Tientsin ratified and carried
out in its original integrity—indemnity for our expenses : it must be your punishment for treachery and
insult—and guarantees against a re-occurrence." This,
nothing but this, when we appear at the mouth of the
Peiho—or the allied armies ought to act at the discre-
tion of their chiefs, until, without comment or discussion, the Emperor is ready to accede to our terms.

If in terms equally simple the alternative be placed
before the Chinaman, and, in terms equally untram-
melled, our naval and military commanders-in-chief be
told what they have to do, much of the difficulty attendant upon the harmonious working of an allied force
will be surmounted; and, what is still more essential,
they will work energetically to a known point, the
plenipotentiary reserving to himself the right, as well
as responsibility of crying Halt ! *when the Emperor, by
duly accredited agents, declares he will comply with
the terms*—and to say Retire ! when every stipulation
that comes immediately into force has been faithfully

carried out. The instructions from England under
which our Admiral and General acted in 1842, after
two years had been spent in a series of operations more
farcical than warlike, were to the effect, that the executive were alone to decide on and carry out hostile
operations in China, without reference to the plenipotentiary, whose responsibility and interference was not
to have effect until such an impression had been made
as would secure a successful negotiation of the terms
laid down. As negotiations can no longer be necessary
for a treaty ratified by our Sovereign and country, and
approved of by the Emperor of China, the stand-point
for hostilities may now be made more explicit, and the
action of the executive still better defined.

But, in the name of all past experience, do not let us
have a serio-comic expedition—flags of truce—fights
and diplomatic conferences alternating ; they lead but
to dilatory proceedings—waste of life (for more, far
more, die by the climate than by the sword in Chinese
wars)—disgust of the executive, discontent and recri-
mination ; and if a Treaty is signed under such circumstances, it is simply an infernal machine which
explodes when least expected.

The history of our Chinese war from 1839 to 1841
ought to be studied by those who advocate such a repetition of a solemn farce—destructive only to those
gallant battalions of the Cameronians, Royal Irish, and

55th Regiments, who lie in the pestilential rice-swamps of Chusan, or the sailors who found their resting-place in the muddy waters of Southern China. I will not consider such proceedings possible, but take it for granted that a course of energetic action has been decided on before so many gallant men were sent to China, and so much treasure has been spent, and that it is a mere fear of the vested interests before referred to that prevents it being boldly avowed.

Let us hope that the splendid fleets and armies of England and France, assembling off the entrance of the Yang-tze River, are but the crusaders of European and Christian civilisation, about to execute the behests of that Providence who, by a series of events unsought by us, has already often called the armed Englishman to pave the way for a better condition of things amongst the benighted millions of the wonderful East.

The south-west, or summer monsoon, is now blowing fresh along all the shores of China ; the difficulty will be, not to get to the Gulf of Pecheli, but, on the contrary, when there, to get back to the south until the north-east monsoon sets in. The Admirals will therefore have, in advancing, to see there is nothing left undone behind them ; and we cannot help thinking that a force of small active vessels, with an expeditionary corps, will have to be formed for the purpose of ascending the Yang-tze-kiang, and operating upon that great artery. Its duties, rather than constituent parts, we will point to. Such a flying force may have to fight at Silver Island, if it is true that that, the only defensible point in the whole river between the Poyang Lake and Shanghai, is now being fortified; but having mastered that difficulty, the southern entrance of the Grand Canal will be in our hands, and the communications and supplies from the rich province of Chekiang, as well as Fokien, be intercepted, and under no circumstances will the capital be then provisioned except we permit it. From Nankin to Ngan-kin they will pass through a rich valley, 100 miles long, once the garden of China, but now devastated by the Taeping hordes, who are not likely to interfere with our forces, seeing that the late Captain Charles Barker, of H.M.S. Retribution, punished them effectually very recently for firing upon our flag, and a solitary gunboat has subsequently cruised amongst them scathless. Between Ngan-kin and the Poyang Lake there are no points likely to be fortified, and at that lake our vessels would intercept the great north and south, or meridian road from Pekin to Canton. They would be able to explore that great lake, collect information of the cities and places of trade situated upon its shores. They would let our bumptious Cantonese friends know that there was a way by which our corvettes and gunboats could cut off all that great inland traffic with the north, of which they have hitherto

had such a monopoly, and which they fancy is out of
the reach of the strong arm of England ; and lastly,
this force would explore for the merchant and missionary the three great provinces, otherwise quite inacces-
sible, of Ki-angsi, Ngan-whuy, and Hupeh.

We would not have this squadron act otherwise
than as an armed reconnoissance, except that they stop
all trade up the Grand Canal. At the same time, the
officers commanding might be instructed not to mislead the people with an idea that we were not at war
with their Emperor, but tell them that by fine, ransom,
or direct hostilities, we were prepared to put down
anything like support of his war-policy. With the
Taepings we ought to be simply neutral. The most
advanced point to which this force would reach would
only be four hundred and fifty miles up the river,
which is the distance from the Light Ship to the
Poyang Lake. H.M.S. Furious and Cruiser descended
the Yang-tze from that point, with the river very low,
in a week ; and if peace be suddenly obtained, and our
commanders-in-chief desired to recall a force so detached, the overland runners from Shanghai would
reach them in considerably less time. Supplies could
be sent them up the stream from Shanghai, and of
fresh meat, fresh vegetables, and fresh water, they
would find no lack in the country they would traverse.

This force would act likewise very beneficially, if

the resistance in the north was greater than is generally anticipated, and enable active operations to be
pushed in one direction, whilst the severity of a Pekin
winter will, if all we are told of it be true, confine
soldiers and sailors to their quarters. Fever and ague
will, however, be the greatest enemy and difficulty of
a force so detached—sickness rather than mortality
being sadly rife in the autumn on the Yang-tze.
Directly the bracing north-east monsoon sets in, this
malady disappears if the men have good clothing ; but
I believe that the malady itself may be almost warded
off by giving the men a generous dietary, varied as
much as possible, and by not keeping them cooped up
on board a ship for month after month. With a little
fun, variety, and occasional excitement, it is wonderful
how healthy our men may be kept in a very delete-
rious climate ; and of course, if the Imperial troops
should take it into their heads to pit gingals and bows
and arrows against Enfield rifles and Armstrong guns,
both Jack the sailor and Joe the marine will infallibly
keep in very excellent health. When sailors suffer,
get sick, and perish, it is when they are idle, ill-fed, or
fretting for change and excitement.

The Yang-tze-kiang and the southern entrance of
the canal being provided for, and the force so detached
being available for any crisis that may occur in Southern China, we will again turn our attention to the

north.   Our fleet will sail four hundred miles over a
veritably Yellow Sea, in soundings constantly, although
no land be seen ; they will be passing over a great continent which the rivers Yang-tze and Hoang are hourly
adding to, and which will in time arise, by constant
accumulation, to the surface, and form a great projection — another Kiang-soo — projecting towards the
Corea and Japan.   The lead sinks deep into it—a
fine, rich, fat alluvium, intended by Providence to
grow fine tea and silk for generations and nations yet
to come.   After the fleet crosses the 35th parallel of
north latitude, they sight the swelling hills of Eastern
Shantung—a block of detached mountainous country
situated in the same parallel of latitude as Caboul and
Armenia, and not unlike those regions in the extremes
of heat and cold to which it is subject—those extremes
modified, however, by Eastern Shantung projecting
into a sea which washes three-fourths of its sea-coast.
This country is the natural base for operations in
Northern China ; without advancing a mile beyond
it, the sea-communication between the capital and the
south will be interrupted ; and it has ports, and we
know not of a single one elsewhere throughout all the
shores of Pecheli and Kiang-soo.   Very little of the
coast of Shantung is as yet known ; but where it
has been visited, anchorages have been found to abound,

and the resources and character of the valleys promise
very fairly for the support of our fleet and army. In
Chefoo Bay the French forces will, we hear, rendezvous. It is situated on the northern face of the Promontory of Shantung, and half-way between Alceste
Point and the entrance of the Gulf of Pecheli. It
is a place of some trade, especially with the Corean
Empire; and although thought to be unsafe in 1858,
appears by recent surveys to have merited a better
character. The British fleet, it is said, will rendezvous
on the Corean coast, at a port recently discovered
in that remarkable projection known as the Regent's
Sword, or called by the natives Lao-thie-shan. That
position appears an excellent one, and is actually at
the entrance of the Gulf; and we may hope that as
that anchorage is actually in the Corea, it may lead to
our receiving some information of that extraordinary
empire, and maybe enable us to open it likewise to
European civilisation and commerce.

When the descent upon the shores of Pecheli, however, takes place, the depots and base will have to be
as near as possible to the scene of action, and then,
maybe the magnificent roadstead under the Mea-tou
islands will be thronged with our transports and
victuallers, and probably upon one of them will be
established—or at any rate near there, on the Tang-

chow-foo Promontory—the depots of stores, the re-
serves of cattle, horses, and munitions of war, as well
as the hospitals of the Allied forces.

Whilst all departments are energetically preparing to fulfil their respective vocations when called
upon, whilst our naval officers are exploring and sur-
veying every creek and bay of the neighbourhood, and
the ultimatum of the Court of Pekin is coming, the
months of June and July will have doubtless sped;
and we need not regret it ;—a heat which paralyses a
native, you may thrust hot fresh Europeans into for a
day's hard fighting, and take them out again to sea;
but leave them to fester under it, in fatigue-parties,
heavy marches, or night-duties as sentinels and pickets,
and they fall like sheaves of corn before a scythe.

In 1858, the thermometers ranged on board the
ships anchored off the Peiho River from 62° to 86°
during June, and from 73° to 98° during July. In
the cool and shady Residency of the Embassy at Tientsin, the range, when our countrymen gladly left it,
was 96° to 71°, and during the last three days it never
fell below 80° Fahrenheit. Our soldiers and sailors
were not then unhealthy, it is true, but that was because they had nothing to do except to eat, drink, and
grow fat, with the perfect conviction that they were
victorious Britons, whom the Emperor of China was
much beholden to for their forbearance, the nourish-

ment of whom the mandarins of Tientsin were especially honoured in looking to, and that the little China boy, whom the sentry at the Embassy had for the time enslaved to fan the flies away from his jolly-looking Somersetshire visage, was doing no more than he came into the world to do. Of course such *luxe* cannot be enjoyed every day, and our admirals or generals are not likely to go to the Peiho in 1860 expecting that state of things to be all ready awaiting the good pleasure of his men, unless he first takes the precaution to thrash Prince Sung-o-losin and his army; and we hardly think Admiral Hope's last reception is likely to mislead him on that point.

We will suppose that the gentry of the Hwashana and Kweiliang stamp, the soothers and betrayers of barbarians, are disposed of, and operations commenced in earnest. In the month of August the nights will be cooler, and the men will sleep well and awake refreshed from the heats of the day. There are twelve weeks left for active hostilities, and to secure themselves before winter! The Gulf of Pecheli is said to be unnavigable in winter, and probably freezes over as the Baltic and Sea of Azov do, from the 14th November to the 14th January. If it is decided that Tientsin shall be taken, garrisoned, and held throughout the winter, there will be plenty to do, even if the resistance be but small; and, strategically speaking, its immediate possession is of the utmost importance. With it and the seaboard we must hold the supply of Pekin in our hands, and if anything short of the capture of Pekin can bring the Emperor to his senses, those measures, accompanied by a thorough and effectual defeat of his army, ought to do it. Apart from the fall of Tientsin, and the destruction of the Taku forts, there are many places easily accessible to our forces, where a severe lesson to the capital may be read, and in almost close propinquity to it. Funingfoo, as well as Chang-lai, great walled cities, lie on the shores of the Gulf of Pecheli northward of the Peiho. The former drives a considerable trade in grain with Shinking *via* Neu-chang, and it will doubtless be necessary to make our presence felt by temporary occupation and ransom of every accessible city along the shore of the Pecheli province, before the winter sets in, so as to increase the pressure upon the capital, and divert from it those supplies which it would otherwise insist upon.

Tientsin, once in our hands, is as capable of defence against an enemy as it would now be a formidable place to attack if it were garrisoned by Europeans. The Peiho River and the canal intersect the city and suburbs into three distinct masses, so that on whichever side you approach it, a huge ditch has to be twice crossed before the entire place can fall into the hands of the victor. A light iron tramroad and locomotive engine would be invaluable in carrying to Tientsin from Taku such supplies during the winter as may not then be in depot there. Of course the Peiho River will be frozen over, and impracticable to our gunboats long before the Gulf is : indeed, there is some reason to doubt whether the lower part of the Gulf—that is, between the Peiho River and the Mea-tou Isles—is ever frozen over, although it may be encumbered with drift ice from the rivers, as well as the head of the Gulf. Taku I should therefore consider as always accessible to our steamers ; and if the surface of the Peiho River becomes, as I doubt not, firmly frozen over, there will be a natural and excellent causeway over its surface up to Tientsin. One of the phenomena, spoken of by the junkmen, during the winter time, was the blowing away of the water in shallow parts of the Gulf. It only requires for our seamen to be aware of this to guard against it ; but it is a sure proof of the great violence of the wintry gales in the Gulf of Pecheli. The missionary Gutzlaff mentions experiencing the effects of wind upon the water of the Gulf many years ago. I should perhaps think more of it had I and my comrades, in the Sea of Azov in 1855-56, not experienced it to a great extent, and found that it required the same precautions to guard against being wrecked under such circumstances as you would employ if anchored in a strange place with great fall of tide.

General report declares the winter of Pecheli to be very severe; I believe it, although it puzzles me to explain how it is so, when the whole face of the country is covered with a half-naked, half-starving working class of population, such as I have described in an earlier page.

There is every reason to believe that provisions have been and can be thrown into the capital by some route which leads across Shantung, from ports on its south-east coast which have yet to be discovered, and soldiers and sailors will have plenty to do, during the cold bracing weather, in exploring a country as large as England, Scotland, and Wales, and, we fancy, not unlike them in physical features and products. Perhaps the secret which the Chinese have as yet so well kept of where the Yellow River is now discharging itself will likewise be unravelled, and some of our gallant little gunboats show the Chinaman that his troublesome stream is a mere pigmy to the giant steam. Should the spring—the early spring of 1861— still find the Emperor recalcitrant, the war party in Pekin still obstinate—and, looking to the encouragement both have received in certain quarters at home, such a contingency is far from unlikely—the army will then be in an excellent position to advance upon

Pekin, and taking Tung-chow on their way, encamp
in the "Palace of the Earth's Repose" until better
sense returns to the "Halls of intense mental exercises," or that of "Heavenly rest."

A deliberate steady approach of this character will
have, in my opinion, a far more lasting effect on the
Court, and every Chinaman be disabused of his present
prevalent idea, that we are going to make a rush,
create a panic, "that Emperor he go Zehol, you
no can stay Pekin, you come again down this Can-
tonne side, allo samee before, allo man sabe that
fashion!" and that if they are only obstinate, and
sacrifice a few tens of thousands of poor creatures by
hunger and want, we shall gladly give up all that is
worth having in our new Treaty, and go back into the
old groove, having wasted millions, and lost hundreds
of good men, without having broken down, as we
before said, the unrighteous walls of monopoly which
bar out four hundred millions of men from European
civilisation and God's truth.

Two questions may arise in the minds of those who
read the opinions I have expressed upon our probable
course of action at Tientsin. They may ask whether I
believe that the occupation of Tientsin will give us
peace, and induce the Emperor to fulfil his engagements, and grant such farther demands as we may
deem necessary. I have no hesitation in saying, "No."

The terrible long delay in visiting the treachery of Taku with punishment, has had the worst effect in the North of China, and if they give us our old Treaty again at Tientsin after a fight at Taku—and fight they will, unless we eat an amazing lot of diet—I would not give the price of old paper stuff for it.

Then why not go direct to Pekin, and at once? will be asked. My reply is, Because you have to go there arm-in-arm with our friends over the water. *Coup-de-mains* are simply impossible in Allied operations; and a *coup-de-main*, to be of use, must, moreover, be unexpected. Now, a rush at Pekin is just what the Chinese expect; they have been threatened with it so long that they know it will come, and they have taken good counsel upon the subject. I do not believe they intend to contest our entry, but simply to hand it over, whilst the Court goes off where it goes annually for some months, into Manchouria. They calculate that with a long winter before us, our supplies, 160 miles off outside the bar of the Peiho River, and two millions of starving inhabitants around us, we should soon be sick of our prize, and I rather agree with them. If we had been at Taku in early spring, we might make the experiment, because before winter our force would be secured; but the experiment in August, with winter due in ninety days, is quite another thing. At any rate, I for one will not counsel the measure ; those on the spot may possibly see cause to justify them in such a *coup* at Pekin ; if they do attempt it, we can only hope that the result may be advantageous.

A letter from a friend at Shanghai says that—" Ever since the spring set in at Pekin, the Court has been sending off caravans ladened with valuables, out of the way of our expected visit, although Prince Sung-o-losin maintains he can beat back any number of us into the sea. When we go to Pekin, therefore, go deliberately, and in force, and with such supplies as will show the Emperor you will hold it until he really comes to his senses. If you do this, we may only have to go there once instead of several times."

One word more. A guarantee against a re-occurrence of hostilities and gross treachery, though difficult to obtain, is essential. We would suggest that, in the first place, the reconstruction of the Taku forts be objected to ; that a position be selected as near the Peiho River as possible for the establishment of a European factory or settlement — the consuls exercising within the limits of their respective factories magisterial functions (the Mea-tou Islands would probably afford such a position) ; no fortifications to be erected by Europeans, except in self-defence against the Chinese ; and that it shall be considered a neutral spot in European wars. Its proximity to Pekin would check that court, if it contemplated any farther duplicity; it would be a place of refuge for our merchants or diplomatists resident in Pecheli; and the cession of such an island or spot to the Allies would have the most marked effect upon the Chinese and Manchous of Northern China—would form a tangible proof of our success, and of the punishment awaiting breaches of treaty engagements.

I grant that the slower and surer process which I advocate will be more expensive at the outset, than a rush which would temporarily bewilder the slow-thinking mandarins; but we have had an instance already of how soon they recover their wits, and open with a view-halloo upon a new war. The expense, I maintain, of our present operations ought and should fall upon the Chinese government, not upon the English people. I have already pointed out one source from whence indemnity can be secured without effecting any of the acknowledged sources of imperial revenue. The Emperor of the French has, we learn by the last mails, insisted, through his representative, upon indemnity for his war expenses; we have, in a half-hesitating manner, followed suit. Napoleon III. is perfectly right; and will it not be strange if France really recovers her indemnity, whilst we magnanimously screw it out of our countrymen instead of Chinamen? Yet I believe it far from unlikely—because in China and at

home there is a certain set who have far more sympathy for "the poor benighted heathen," than for the
hard-working Christians in their own country—people
who are always trying to legislate for Turk, Hindoo, or
Chinaman, instead of looking to the well-being alone
of their own compatriots. I perfectly appreciate the
policy of not killing the goose that lays golden eggs;
but in this question of indemnity, I am confident that
we shall read the Chinese a lesson by insisting upon it,
which would have more effect than the occupation of
one-half their cities, or the slaughter of a million of
their countrymen. If we desired territorial com-
pensation, I grant that the cession of territory would
have as good an effect ; but we want not territory,
we simply require to be paid back what has been
fairly spent in bringing them to reason. The Chancellor of the Exchequer, Mr Gladstone, estimates
the expenses of the rod, which diplomacy is about
to apply to the Emperor Kien-fung's seat of reason,
at about six million and a-half. It is a royally expensive one, considering that the indemnity for the
war of 1840-41-42 only amounted to about four
millions and a-half sterling ; but at any rate, the
sequestration of the Foreign Custom dues received in
China for the next two years would nearly yield the
said six millions, and pay the expenses of administration likewise. Those custom dues are not a legal or

recognised source of imperial revenue in China.
Kwieliang and Hwashana would scorn to allow, as
Lin and Yeh would have done before them, that their
Emperor cared one straw for the revenue derivable
from foreign trade. Intercourse with us in any way
was contrary to tradition, to reason, and to law ; we
insist upon it, and they naturally "squeeze us" as
a penalty. We pay the squeezes willingly, because
we hope that in time they will see that our trade is of
importance to the imperial resources ; but I do not
see why we should allow those resources to be devoted to defeating the very object we now have in
view, an extension of our commerce and a lasting peace
with China. If we had to seek in 1860 for any fresh
concessions from the Emperor Hien-fung, relative to
opening ports, or other points which would eventually
secure for us advantages commercial or political, I
should say, forego the indemnity, and obtain them ; we
shall repay ourselves by increased trade and revenue.
Lord Elgin, in 1858, acted upon that principle ; he
set indemnity on one side in order to secure advantages that were of fourfold value ; the concessions
he then obtained go to Chinese credit against all the
expense and trouble we were put to during 1856, 1857,
and 1858. But it is not so in the present case, and I
urge most earnestly that we now make the Chinese
smart in the only way you can touch their feelings,

through their pockets; and although I have taken the
trouble to show how it can be done, I do so merely to
prove my statement that they have abundant resources
in China—not because I think we have any reason to
consult their convenience upon the matter. It is the
fashion to talk of the Chinese government as being
poor and weak. There is sentiment about it which
harmonises with the idiosyncrasy of the Englishman;
everybody is a poor beggar but ourselves and Brother
Jonathan. Take any man fresh from 'Change, and drop
him in the fusty, foul city of Shanghai, and he would
fancy he was amongst a collection of Eastern paupers.
He would be long discovering the extraordinary wealth
and importance of that city and its traders. If he
had seen the Imperial Commissioners, Kweiliang and
Hwashana, one of them the second officer of that vast
empire, he would have seen them, living in a state of
tawdry dirt, surrounded by mean-looking retainers, and
exhibiting wealth only at their meals, where there were
abundant proofs that all quarters of the globe were contributing to their creature comforts. If our Englishman had entered even an imperial yamun, he would
have been struck with the absence of all that we con-
nect with wealth. Dust, mildew, and bats, mixed up
with carved granite, jade-stone, and gilt. This is simply China, for there, as in the East generally, men do
not parade their riches, lest they be taken from them.

China is very rich; the indemnity of 1842, some
thirty million dollars, or six millions sterling, was a
mere flea-bite out of the coffers of a nation that has
been hoarding from all time—ever selling to the
foreigner, seldom purchasing. Since that day she has
tripled the sale of her produce to Great Britain alone,
her people have actually entered into competition with
us as traders in our own colonies, and with very great
success, carrying back their accumulated fortunes to the
land of their birth. The Chinese resident in Singapore and the Straits of Malacca are actually purchasing European vessels and running against us in the
Archipelago, as well as in the coasting trade of China,
in Chinese steamers. Does this, I ask, look like
national bankruptcy?—national poverty? At the same
time, we know that the government of China can exercise almost despotic power over the people, and that it
has levied vast sums, as well as material, wherewith to
erect fortifications, to cast cannon, and pay troops to
resist us. Why they should not be made to do as
much, in order that we may be indemnified for knock-
ing them down, puzzles me.

Before quitting this question of indemnity, I have
merely to point out that the grain trade or tax to
Pekin may be indicated as another source perfectly
accessible to us. We may seize much of that grain,
say one half of it, or 200,000 tons, and that at the

prices ruling in Pecheli province in 1858 would be worth alone four million sterling. The salt-works and stores at Tientsin, which are purely imperial property, would likewise yield a large sum—and thus without any pressure upon the inhabitants, without any razzias or foraging parties, war might be made to support war in China.

War! God save the mark. Let not our countrymen run away with the idea that I or any other naval or military man look upon a war in China as war in its legitimate sense—a field where personal honour or glory are to be won. No; believe me, few who have shared in our operations in China fancy any such thing. The dead there are enshrouded with no fame, the living have brought little away except shattered health—our only reward and consolation must be that we have paved, and shall still pave, the way by the expenditure of life and labour for the advance of Christianity, civilisation, and commerce, and promote the honour and glory of our Queen and country.

Standing, as I did in 1858, amongst those ruined graves where hecatombs of my gallant countrymen lie in a festering valley of Chusan, the victims of 1840, 1841, and 1842; knowing as I did, that though their bones lay there exposed, a prey to the wild-dog, and a disgrace to their Christian fellow-men—within a few

M

miles of their poor dust, the great commercial emporium of Shanghai had sprung into existence, and
that not far off had risen Hong-Kong, with its 70,000
inhabitants, its palaces, and wealth, I felt indeed that
my comrades had not died in vain, and that in time
to come the historian of British progress in the East
will not fail to do honour collectively to those servants
of her Crown, who have been her pioneers in that
distant land of Cathay.   That must be our reward, and
is our true incentive to exertion as a profession.   A
sketch in a recent work upon China, written by a
mercantile man evidently, depicts a group of naked,
half-starved, undersized creatures, as " Our Enemies
in China."   The statement is neither witty, just to our
forces, nor true.   The starving-industrious or money-
making animals (for they are little better) constituting
the masses in China, are not our enemies, nor are we
theirs—at least if we are, so is the missionary, and so
is the merchant.   We are the representatives of a
nation which is civilising, improving, and, I hope, will
one day Christianise those creatures.   They find everywhere in us kind and just masters ; there can be no
enmity between us.   No ! our enemy—that is, the
enemy of British Progress in China—is he who stands
between us and these creatures—the burly, obstinate,
over-fed mandarins, the Yehs, the Lins, of Chinese

bureaucracy, the vain self-sufficient literati, and above all, those traders ; *and they are not all Chinamen though they think like them,* who would sacrifice everything rather than forego their profits, or risk their wretched monopoly.

APPENDIX.

MEMORANDA extracted from *Travels in China* (by Sir John Barrow, Bart.), relative to the PEIHO RIVER and the PROVINCE of PECHELI, between Taku and Pekin.

I EXPERIENCED so much difficulty in obtaining information about the neighbourhood of Pekin, that I have thought right, for the sake of those now labouring in China, to annex some scraps of information from the writings of the late Secretary of the Admiralty, which will be of much use to our soldiers and sailors, and of interest to those who have friends and relations in the present allied expedition. Speaking of the lower portion of the Peiho River, Sir John says that the land on both sides was low and flat. There were few trees except near the villages, which were of a mean appearance. And although the villages were numerous, no assemblage of houses worthy of the name of a town was perceived. Everything, in fact, wore an air of poverty and meanness, and was deeply disappointing to those who had formed exaggerated notions of what would be seen in the neighbourhood of the capital of one of the greatest empires in the world. The embassy, however, were struck with the vast multitudes which daily flocked down to look upon the strangers; but their general appearance

indicated a want of comfort and happiness.   The weather
was extremely sultry, the temperature ranging at 88°
Fahr. in the shade, and this in the month of August.
The observations made by the Embassy show a ther-
mometric range during August, of from 80° to 88° during the day, and during the night from 60° to 64°.   In
September the medium temperature during the day fell to
76°, and in October to 68°; but in the latter month the
thermometer fell at night to 44° Fahr.

Above Tientsin, the Peiho was considerably contracted
in dimensions, and the stream more powerful.   The surface of the country began to be less uniform in appearance, partially broken into hill and dale, but nothing ap-
proaching to a mountain anywhere visible.   It was, however, still scantily wooded, few trees appearing except large
willows on the banks of the river, and knots of elms or
firs about the temples or public buildings.   In the neighbourhood of the navigable part of the Peiho River—namely,
from Taku to Tung-chow—a light sandy soil prevails, with
a mixture of argillaceous earth and slimy matter inter-
spersed with shining particles of mica; but not a stone of
any magnitude, nor pebbles, nor even gravel, was observed.

During all August and September the Embassy only
experienced one shower of rain, the sky generally cloud-
less.   In October, when the Embassy returned to Tientsin
from Tung-chow, they embarked in vessels very different
from those in which they had ascended the stream two
months previously—the river having fallen so much as to
compel the Chinese to employ vessels singularly shallow
and flat-bottomed ; yet Barrow speaks of them as sufficiently commodious.   Barrow dwells upon the scarcity of
draught animals, but speaks of having seen the following

vegetables and cereals under cultivation : Cabbages, carrots, turnips, radishes, coarse asparagus, melons, pumpkins, cucumbers, and a profusion of onions and garlic. The fruits were tolerable—peaches, indifferent apples, not unlike quinces, and pears of an immense size, but very tasteless. Two species of millets, different sorts of kidney beans, a few patches of buck-wheat ; but neither buck-wheat, barley, nor oats.

It is worthy of note that Barrow estimated the distance from Taku to Tientsin as about *ninety* miles in distance, and from Tientsin to Tung-chow as about *eighty* miles more. Now we know that this estimate of the length of the stream from the sea to Tientsin is more than double what it really is—a very natural error when we remember that the Embassy, of which Barrow was a member, made a voyage in a junk which had often to be tracked. But, as he over-estimated the length of the one stage, we may justly infer that he did as much for the other portion of his tedious journey, and that the Peiho River, above the city of Tientsin, will not be so tortuous as we suppose ; and that the distance between Tientsin and Tung-chow is considerably under ninety miles—probably not more than forty geographical miles.

Speaking of the road between Tung-chow and Pekin, Barrow says that it led across an open country, sandy and ill-cultivated. The middle of the road, for the width of 18 or 20 feet, was paved with stones of granite from 6 to 16 feet in length, and broad in proportion.

Of Pekin externally we are told that none of the buildings overtopped the walls, although the walls did not appear to exceed 25 or 30 feet in height. Square bastions projected at every 70 yards from the walls ; each bastion had a small guardhouse on the summit. The thickness of the wall was about 25 feet at the base, and 12 feet on the parapet, the walls sloping considerably, and consisting of brick and stone, enclosing a mass of earth. No cannon were seen.

Sir John Barrow says the city is an oblong square, the enclosing walls being equal to about 14 English miles in extent. In the south wall there are three gates—in the other sides only two. The centre gate on the south side communicates directly with the imperial palaces, or portion of the capital reserved to the use of the Emperor and his family. Between the other two gates and corresponding ones on the north side, run two streets, perfectly straight, about four miles long and 120 feet wide. One street of a similar width runs from one of the eastern to one of the western gates of Pekin. The other streets of Pekin are merely narrow lanes, branching from and connecting these great streets. At the four angles of the city walls four storied pagodas were observed; and at the points of intersection of the four great streets, buildings of a similar description were seen. None of the streets were in any way paved—the narrow lanes appeared to be watered, but the great ones were covered with sand and dust.

Such are the general features of Pekin: they are doubly valuable, scant as they are, as the observations of an eyewitness. In the *Canton Repository* and in Mr William's *Middle Kingdom* there are more details and plans of the interior of the city; but as they, the facts, are drawn from Chinese authority, and some of them at direct variance with the statements of European visitors, I think their value doubtful, and hardly worth transcribing.

There are one or two additional facts in Barrow's work

worthy of notice. Between Tientsin and Tung-chow he actually counted more than 1000 vessels, of a large size, each containing ten or twelve distinct apartments built upon their decks, each vessel containing on an estimate fifty persons; and what with these large barges, and all the various river craft met with in that portion of the Peiho River, the British Embassy concluded that at least 100,000 souls were living upon the stream, either on pleasure or business.

Huge granaries belonging to the government were observed in the suburbs of Pekin, immediately outside the walls. Those granaries are now reported to be established at Tung-chow. The imperial government sell this grain to the traders of Pecheli, and the expenses of the court are defrayed out of the proceeds. It was noticed that the houses were constructed to avoid the bitter north winds of the winter. All dwellings on the plains faced the south; and great suffering from cold amongst the poorer classes during the winter was generally asserted. In the middle of October the junks were securing and preparing for winter. A Dutch Embassy which visited Pekin in the winter time found all the rivers and canals frozen solid, and the temperature for thirty-six days " was seldom higher than 10° or 12° below the freezing-point."

THE END.

PRINTED BY WILLIAM BLACKWOOD AND SONS, EDINBURGH.

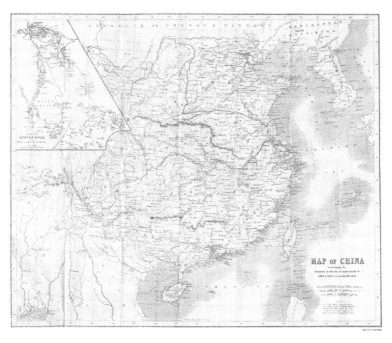

The material originally positioned here is too large for reproduction in this reissue. A PDF can be downloaded from the web address given on page iv of this book, by clicking on 'Resources Available'.

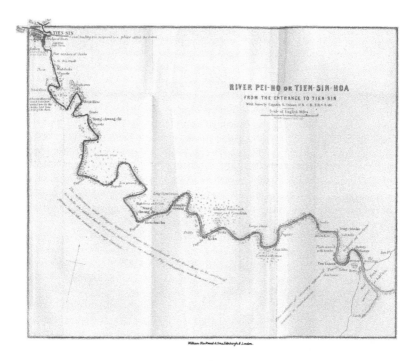

RIVER PEI-HO or TIEN-SIN-HOA

FROM THE ENTRANCE TO TIEN-SIN

The material originally positioned here is too large for reproduction in this reissue. A PDF can be downloaded from the web address given on page iv of this book, by clicking on 'Resources Available'.

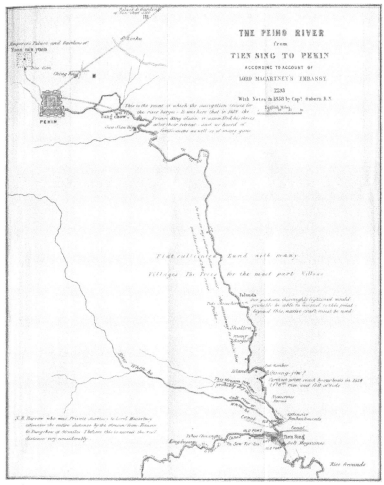

The material originally positioned here is too large for reproduction in this reissue. A PDF can be downloaded from the web address given on page iv of this book, by clicking on 'Resources Available'.

For EU product safety concerns, contact us at Calle de José Abascal, 56–1°,
28003 Madrid, Spain or eugpsr@cambridge.org.

www.ingramcontent.com/pod-product-compliance
Ingram Content Group UK Ltd.
Pitfield, Milton Keynes, MK11 3LW, UK
UKHW012345130625
459647UK00009B/531